FAMILY

ALSO BY J. CALIFORNIA COOPER

A Piece of Mine
Homemade Love
Some Soul to Keep

J. CALIFORNIA COOPER

family

a novel

DOUBLEDAY

New York   London   Toronto   Sydney   Auckland

PUBLISHED BY DOUBLEDAY

a division of Bantam Doubleday Dell
Publishing Group, Inc.
666 Fifth Avenue,
New York, New York 10103

DOUBLEDAY and the portrayal of an
anchor with a dolphin are trademarks
of Doubleday, a division of
Bantam Doubleday Dell, Inc.

Book Design by Gina Davis

Library of Congress Cataloging-in-Publication Data

Cooper, J. California.
Family : a novel / J. California Cooper. — 1st ed.
p.   cm.
1. Afro-American women—History—
Fiction.   I. Title.
PS3553.O5874F36   1991
813'.54—dc20   90-36996   CIP
ISBN 0-385-41171-5

ACKNOWLEDGMENTS

To all those of you who have encouraged and supported me. I need that.

My daughter, Paris, who lifts me with her support and love.

My sister, Shy, who actually reads my work!

Warren D. Smith, who runs hither and yon, doing things for me so I will have the peace and support to do my work.

To Robbie Lee of Black Heritage Art Gallery in Houston, who saves and points out all those beautiful, emotion-filled paintings to me. They provoke new thoughts and give me more people to tell about and love.

To Temma Kaplan, Barnard College, for her large, generous kind heart full of thoughtful doings. Barbara Tatum, Barnard College, for her sweet, thoughtful kindnesses.

Amistad Bookplace of Houston, Texas. Thank you, Rosa and Denice, for all the valuable help you have given me.

To Reid Boates, and Karen and the two little sons that make Reid the most wonderful man/agent I know.

To the wonderful people of my last publisher—Michael Denneny, Michelle Hinkson, Sarah, Keith—all of them who were, and are, always so considerate and kind.

To the most wonderful new people of my new publisher, Doubleday—Sallye Leventhal, Evelyn Hubbard, Arabella, Heidi, Tina, Nancy, and others—with their encouragement, faith, and yes, thoughtful kindnesses. I hope never to let them down. Martha Levin too!

To Jehovah God. Oh, what would I do without Him?

F A M I L Y

AND THE EARTH MOTHER ASKED
THE EARTH CHILD AS SHE HANDED IT
THE SUCCULENT EARTH FRUIT, "AND
WHEN DOES A TREE BEAR FRUIT THAT
IS NOT ITS OWN?"

AND THE EARTH CHILD THREW
BACK ITS BEAUTIFUL HEAD, LAUGH-
ING, SAYING, "NEVER, NEVER . . ."
THEN TOOK A HUGE BITE FROM THE
HEAVY FULL FRUIT WHICH SENT THE
RICH JUICE RUNNING DOWN ITS CHIN,
FALLING, FALLING OVER THE MOUN-
TAINS OF THE EARTH CHILD. ROLL-
ING, ROLLING DOWN AND INTO THE
RIVER OF LOVE AND HATE CALLED
TEARS. RUNNING, RUNNING EVEN
OVER THE FIELDS OF TIME, UNTIL ALL
THE JUICES FLOWED TOGETHER AGAIN,
BLENDING, INTO THE OCEAN OF HU-
MAN LIFE.

THE SUN LOOKED DOWN . . . THE
MOON PEERED UP. LISTENING, MOV-
ING ON, SAYING, "EVERYONE KNOWS
THAT. THAT'S WHAT MAKES A
FAMILY!"

CHAPTER 1

HISTORY. LIVED, NOT WRITTEN, is such a thing not to understand always, but to marvel over. Time is so forever that life has many instances when you can say "Once upon a time" thousands of times in one life.

There was a time, long, long ago, when a little man, Egyptian and Greek, came floating up the Nile working on a water vessel going to upper Egypt. With him, another man of African and Italian blood was working his way home to Africa. Upon reaching the end of the Nile, they were friends, and decided to travel on to Africa together with a caravan. They were yet poor, buying one donkey to share between them, when they started across the Sudan. I can see even now the waves of heat from the close, close sun, rising from the earth's vast sands, enveloping them. They, in their turbans and clean, ragged robes, looking straight ahead toward their home.

Upon reaching the friend's home and family, the little man looked and fell in love with his friend's sister. In time, in spite of her family's desires, they married. They moved farther down into Africa to live. They had children. After many years, their children had children. And so on and so on.

Came the time when the slave catchers came. Some of the couple's living children were taken. Stolen, separated and taken to many lands . . . sold. A few lived on. They had children. These children had children by their owners and others. Portuguese, Spanish, English, Italian, French, Irish, Scottish, others. Men from lands all over the world. Until one day, near my time, a girl-child was born who was to be my grandmother. In time, my mother was born. She lived and was sold, yet again. That is where I was to come from. Ahhh, how sad, how sad for all of us.

So, once upon another time, a long, long time ago, time didn't mean anything to my people, exceptin it was hard times all the time. And time can look endless. That's the time I was born.

Some people say we was born slaves . . . but I don't blive that. I say I was born a free human being, but I was made a slave right after.

There was only one person in my family I knew at that time. My mother. We knew we blonged together cause she had birthed me. Didn't know my daddy. Well, we knew him but wasn't lowed to tell it and I couldn't call him daddy, when I was able to talk. Didn't have no grandmothers livin that we knew of, or nothin like that. Mama said she knew her mama had some kin in Africa somewhere, but we didn't know where and they didn't know nothin bout us now, nohow. See . . . her grandmama had been most jet black in her color. Or was it her grandmama's mother? Anyway, I do know we did start out bein black. Just no family, cept just us, my mother and me, and we wasn't together too much cept in the nights and some most of them the Master of the Land came in and pushed me over and out the bed. I'd lay there on the floor with my eyes closed, suckin my thumbs til he was gone. Then she be mine again. I would rock her to sleep and myself too. I cried cause she cried. We was both tired of the life we was livin. I wasn't nothin but a baby-child but I was still tired of things I didn't even know what name to call em.

My mother had nine more children for the Master of the Land, but they was all sold when they got to be bout three years old by the Mistress of the Land cause they was too white and lookin like the Master of the Land. That, and the money.

See . . . my mama had me by a black man so she could have her a brown baby. She wouldn't tell who my daddy was so they wouldn't hurt him or sell him cause they hadn't been let to do no lovin together. She said they was in love but that wasn't lowed. They didn't get to be in love no-more tho cause she was watched hard. And I got punished extra lots. And I was even still his property, even if I wasn his own child!

My mama was very light cause her father had been a Master of the Land. That's why I didn't have no grandmother on her side cause Grandmother had killed herself rather than stay in slavery and keep on bringing more babies into the world to be made more slaves or whatever anybody wanted them to be. That's what I hear tell she said.

Cause my mama hated white folks, she wanted a brown baby. See . . . my daddy being a dark-skinned man made me a tan color or whatever God would call it. But a brown slave or a white colored slave . . . what's the difference? I was about twelve years old when my mama just musta decided she just couldn't take life no more. All her babies gone cept me. (Don't care who the daddy was, they was still her children.) And always havin to harken to the white Master of the Land and get another baby to lose out into anywhere-land, she just couldn't take it no more. See?

The Mistress watched her husband, the Master,

hard, hard, but not hard enough to keep him in her own bed. Cause it's a thousand excuses to be out the house on a country farm that size. And when my mama gave birth to another white baby the Mistress of the Land wouldn't hate her husband, uh, uh, she would hate my mama more. And, this the truth. I been in that big house, cleaning or somethin like that, when white ladies be talkin and they say that "them nigger womens is sex fiends" or somethin like that and blame it all on the slave women! Just like they wasn't slaves or that they had made them babies all by their own selves . . . or forced them white men!

Anyway . . . my mama had a hard, hard life. All day she blonged to the Mistress for the work in the big house, and in the nights *he* chose, she blonged to the Master. Didn't have her own self no time. A somebody with a mind will surely go crazy like that cause no matter what you think, it don't count for nothin. She didn't have nothin of her own but me, and I blonged to them too. And I could go anytime! They told her that, often. See . . . my mama was pretty and that made the Mistress hate her. And smart . . . that made the Master want to rule her more. They didn't want her to have just what only she was born with. Some of the other slaves didn't like her neither! But my mama was sweet to me.

I remember that special day cause I had worked in the house side my mama washing three tub loads of clothes, big loads, too! Then we both been sent out to the fields to help there too. It was plumb dark when we staggered in, leaning on each other, too tired to eat, almost too tired to sleep had we coulda at that time. I was cryin a little, don't know zackly why cause wasn't nothin really hurtin me, I was just tired . . . just tired. Tired. Maybe it was cause "tomorrow . . . tomorrow" was goin to be just the same thing all over again. A new name for the same day, over and over again. That was what made me feel like cryin. I don't know. I do know we put ourselves down on that cornshuck bed and lay there breathin hard. We had to get up tho, cause we had a few more things to do with feeding the rest of the slaves from the field, foldin those washed clothes, then cleanin up after the slave supper.

It was THAT day the Master of the Land said my mama was goin to go for to be his son's night-mate too, smilin down at her like he was doin her some special kinda good favor.

Now . . . that man's son was young. And the Master had many slaves on his land. He knew my mama was old in her body, even as young as she was sposed to be in years. He had to know my mama was tired. Everybody knows bout work! And bein tired! Ain't that why people try to get somebody else to do their work? People will give you the money they love and hate to part with just to keep from doin their own WORK! Ain't that true? Even now . . . today . . . in your day? See . . . he could have picked somebody else! She done already carried and had nine of his babies what he got good feelin from and good money for!

Why didn't he? I done found out you can't see into nobody's mind no matter what comes out their mouths nor what their actions are. But I know for my own self when somebody don't give a damn bout you and treat you like you ain't nothin. Now I didn't wish nobody else, no other woman, no bad luck, to have to use their body when they don't want to, but, that was my mama . . . and I wisht he had picked somebody else. Later on, I know he wisht he had too! At twelve years old, I was beginnin to understand life, feeling it.

That day she came in from her last jobs and helped me finish mine, washing tin plates for the next morning. Then she took me into that ole dark, broke-down chicken house in the black of the night and held me to her close, close. She squeezed me so tight it hurt my bones cause I was already sore from work, but I loved bein in my mama's arms, so I never said a word. Uh, uh.

She cried . . . and I cried again. I didn't know just what exactly we was cryin bout that time, but there was so many things to cry about it didn't matter.

She rubbed my face, my back and arms. Held me away from her, looked at me and cried harder. I did too, cause who likes to see their mama cry? Lord! Not me.

We finally slowed down cryin. She wiped her eyes, then my eyes, with the tail of her worn-out dress of that ole shitty-color sackcloth. Then she leaned over and drew some lines on the ground. Justa sniffling all the time. I know now there was twelve lines. She say, "That's how old you are, Clora." Her name was Fammy, my name was Clora. I sniffed and said, "Yes mama, mam."

She say, "They gonna count you a woman soon, for sure." I almost smiled cause I thought that might be good but she only cried more, with no sound now. I said, "Yes mam. Don't cry like that, mama." She say, "Lord, I can't help you none, child." I held her tight, said, "Yes you do, mama." She heaved a big sigh, said, "No. I can't help you none, baby. Mama can't even help herself." I held on to her tight.

She looked down at me, rubbed my tears from my eyes, wiped my running nose, said, "No matter whatsomever happens, you remember I loves you. I loves you very hard. You my child." She was squeezin my shoulder and it hurt, but I still didn't do nothin but look up at her. She said, "You always gonna remember that?" I nodded through my tears and I still didn't know exactly why we was cryin this time. But I did not care. Somehow this little piece of time we was havin together was worth anything to me. It was OUR TIME and hadn't nobody appointed it to us. It was just ours and we took it cause we had a mind of our own, even if we did have to hide to use em!

Then we heard those dam-awful footsteps! We knew it was somebody white cause they was walkin in shoes. All the slaves was barefoot, you know that. My mama let loose of me and jumped up knockin her head on some wood cross the door. She never hollered to show her pain, just ran out the chicken house leavin me behind. Some reason I never even got to think of made me just sit in there and cry like my heart was goin to break. I was feelin so low, so sad . . . I couldn't help myself from all those tears. I finally got up and dried my eyes, brushed the dirt and dried chicken dodo off my piece a' clothes and wound my way to our shack in the blackest night I ever been in. See? Life made that night black, not the sky or the sun bein gone. My mama feelin bad and bein hurt, hittin her head, and all that cryin made that night so dark. Sometime, when life be hittin you with a sledgehammer, it don't stop til it done drove you all the way down, far as you can go down . . . to the bottom.

CHAPTER 2

I WAS SO TIRED, so worn out, inside my body and head and outside where my muscles was, I just fell into the bed with them cornshucks just rustling under me. I didn't even wash up or take off my clothes like my mama made me to do. I just wanted to sleep. I was tryin to keep my eyes open til mama came in so I could hold her, make her warm and me too. But I was too tired.

Sleep had drug me so far down til I could feel I was bein shaked but it seemed like it was another world somewhere. I knew it couldn't be, just couldn't be, mornin already. But the shakin kept up and somebody, Miz Elliz, was callin my name. "Clora, Clora child! Wake up! Wake up!" Miz Elliz was the old woman who watched out for the babies while their mamas was in the fields. I pulled with all my might to open my eyes, to move. Then she said, "Clora child, your mama done killed herself! You wake up and come on over to my shack where them other children be. They won't see you there so fast while they mad. She done killed the Master too! Come on now! Child, come on! Heist yourself up and move!" I was wide awake in a second. Cryin again. And scared! I grabbed Miz Elliz's skirts and stumbled after her to her shack and tumbled in with the other slave babies under the raggedy covers. Miz Elliz cautioned with a fierce whisper. "Hush! You be quiet now! Don't . . . you gonna get me in trouble too! Hush!" Then in another moment in a little softer whisper she said, "I know you hurt and you sad . . . cause your mama gone. But if you want to live . . . hush now . . . hush."

I lay in the dark listening to the sounds of the

other children sleepin, thinkin . . . if I want to live. But, I don't want to live. My mama was gone. I didn't have nobody now. Maybe Miz Elliz, but she belonged to everybody the Master told her to keep care of. Then my mind landed on the Master. The Master. The Master wasn't no Master no more. He only was gonna have six feet of land now and he couldn't command nobody to come to where that would be. But that didn't make me feel no better bout my mama. She was gone forever. I even rather have the Master back if I could get Mama back. I wanted to cry, I wanted to scream, I wanted to die. But all I could do is lay there and be still . . . and hush. I found out later when the slaves wasn't scared to whisper bout it that mama had gone to the son like she was ordered to do, but on her way from whatever place that was set up for them to meet, the Master had caught her to ask her about it and his son. They was in the farmyard and she just picked up a pitchfork and stabbed him with it. Then she went somewhere near where they kill the hogs, got her a knife, went back and finished him to death while he screamed for help. No help came cause them slaves wasn't gonna move! They might be blamed for whatever was happening! Then she stabbed herself . . . she was bent double over the fence, bled to death, standin up.

When everything was long over, a month or two, and I could be seen around more in the open again, when the Young Master of the Land needed somebody, he took me. I was still those twelve lines old. I had gone out to that chicken house and got a rock for every line my mama had marked out so I would know my age now that the only other one who would know was gone. So I know I was twelve when he took me. He sneaked so his mama wouldn't know. But when I caught a baby, she knew. She called, only me, that "twelve-year-old slut." She didn't call him nothin but "son." She didn't hate me like she had my mama, tho. Cause, I guess, this was her son, not her husband. I blive she was glad that Ole Master was dead and gone. Yes . . . I was a woman at twelve, and sure was one at thirteen years old when I had my first baby for the Master of the Land.

Even havin him, I still didn't have nobody. You all know that! My mind opened up and I understood my mama. I *was* my mama, now. That's slavery . . . they all alike . . . ain't nothin. I went back to that dark, broken-down chicken house many a day and just sit and think and cry.

My first baby was a very light baby, almost white. Look like a fresh peach. Rosy cream. It was a girl. Lord how I cried for this girl-child right after I got through being glad I had my baby. Thought I had somebody of my own to love and be with. I was a fool! I had forgot that child did not belong to me! And when I thought of her future I pained in my heart. I would hold the little sweet body in my arms, fondle her arms, fingers and hands. Her tiny little ears, her soft little tummy. She would press tiny little rose-petal soft lips to my full breast and kick her strong little legs and feet against my body. I would look at her through tears and love cause I knew SOME-BODY had already decided what her life was to be. How far she could go in life . . . in anything . . . for as long as she drew breath on this earth. THEY had done decided she would never go to school, never learn to read and count, never be married in the right way in front of the Lord and man, never be in love cause she don't know how long fore they be sellin her man-love, never have a new store-bought dress was nice, a new pretty doll . . . just never nothin she wanted.

I looked up to God to talk to him, say something, ask everything . . . but I couldn't find words strong enough to say what I felt. I knew He knew anyway . . . there was many a thousand of me all around this land and I knew they had talked to Him like I wanted to. I didn't look up at Him long tho, cause if these white folks think you prayin you can catch the worstest beatin in your life. See . . . they want Him all to themself too. They want it all! Well, they sure got it! I knew most of em I seen and heard of didn't blive in Him right noway, cause of all the devilish things they would do under them laws they made up for themself. They just used God on us slaves. But I blived if God was Love like I heard read out the Bible, He never made us for to be slaves and suffer like this. And I never did blive they had all God to themselves. I knew He wasn't scared of bein whipped or killed by them if He didn't obey. So I prayed to Him right on, but I did it quiet, inside my head. See . . . some peoples put they heads in big pots when they prayed, so the sound wouldn't carry out when they spoke out loud. I knew He could hear me no matter which way I prayed, so I did it my way.

Anyway . . . I knew no matter what life had in store for either me or my baby I would love her always. So . . . that's what I named her . . . Always. I mumbled it round the big house so they thought I said somethin like "Alice" or somethin. I don't care what they wrote down. My baby's name was Always. Some folks laughed at that name round the slave shacks. But, I didn't care. It was somethin didn't nobody have but me and my baby . . . was that name. Til I realized one day, people use that word all the time. But, still, I knew what I meant, and they didn't have that!

CHAPTER 3

NOW . . . TIME PASSED by slow and fast all at the same time. Ole Endless Time passed. And when the Young Master of the Land came at me again and again, I found out I wasn't as strong as my mama. I hated him! Ohhhh, I hated him. I never felt love with him or bout him. And the men I coulda loved freely, knew I was hisn so they stayed way from me. And so . . . well, I just hated him. Not only for ownin my body, but for blockin my mind, lettin my heart dry and shrivel up cause it didn't have nothin to do but hate him. And I know he didn't really like me. Sho couldn't love me! He just shove me out when he be through usin me. Didn't never pay no mind to his children by me, cept his son, just counted them as property, to keep for work or sell. My son he paid mind to cause he looked just like him and he was white. He had my son whipped, so hard, so hard, I like to die watchin my son bleed from that whip. See . . . he wanted him to have stripes crost his back and be known to be a slave . . . so he wouldn't run off tryin to be free. My son finally did run off. He was hounded to it. He was only fourteen years old. I couldn't help him and his daddy was killin him. The Young Master had finally married up with a sweet-faced, laughing little lady who mighta tried to be nicer to the slaves if he hadda done right. Some people have evil mean streaks in their souls no matter what happens in their lives. Other people, a few, have kind souls til some other people mess with them so much they can't take much more of nothin and then they get that mean evil streak in them to fight back with. It's a few others we ain't got time to talk bout now. The

Young Mistress told the Young Master, "We will always love only each other. NO slaves to bed with like some other no-account low whites." He agreed cause she was new and his and he loved her. But time kept passing like it does and pretty soon he was at me or somebody again. That Young Mistress took to hating us, and him, and soon after that, life got hard up there in that house and out there in them fields even. She was everywhere where she thought he might be when he wasn't with her. The Old Mistress just laughed to herself as she ate them big chunks of pecan fudgies, cause it was her son, not her husband, and didn't we blong to him? Couldn't he do whatever he wanted with us? Sides, she told her, white women was not ladies if they thought too much of "that." They should be glad if their husbands "relieved" themselves out in the garbage-bin.

Now see? I have noticed how people lie to each other when it suits them. I mean, they will mess with your whole life, your whole mind, just to get some point on their side. That old woman knew what was right and what was wrong! She couldn't have forgot what she had suffered. But she did not expect to have no more nobody to love her again in life so she would pretend . . . that that was the way she had planned it, wanted it. And she would let that young woman suffer, HELP her suffer, cause misery does love company if misery is in a evil-mean body! That ole woman Mistress use to tell the house slaves to come to her with their problems and she would help them with counsel . . . like a mother. Chile, I wouldn't go to her for nothin! None of her lies went for nothin to them house slaves. I went to Miz Elliz. She was almost like family to me and my children. I knew I could trust her for the truth. Time kept passin. Pretty soon Young Mistress had two babies for our Master. I had had six, but only four of mine had done lived. See . . . when I was still very young and had to go into the fields to work, I didn't know much bout keepin babies. They wouldn't let us carry our babies on our backs with us, or nothin. We had to lay them down by the side of the field and leave em there for four or five hours til it was time for us to eat somethin, then we could feed our babies. I laid my first one out there, wrapped in a gunnysack. It was a boy, and he kicked that sack off and lay out there in that bakin sun all them hours. His little tender skin was just bout cooked. He died from them burns. I cried, oh how I cried. You don't want them to grow to be slaves, but you do want your children to grow up.

The next one I lost, I put him up high off the ground in a shade tree and he got bit by a scorpion or a snake. Couldn't save him neither. Yes, lost both of em. As they died, I dug their graves, wrapped them in their gunnysack cloth, and covered them with the land that blonged to the Master. Miz Elliz was the only one had time to be there and she said the few words she knew. "God take this baby wit you." Then it was back, each time, to go on, don't miss a step for the Master. All our babies looked alike. Now . . . that's really something, if one or two is superior and does not show it. But Young Mistress did not realize the greatest difference of all. Ours would be slaves: sold, or used and misused. Hers . . . would not. I could see all my children were going to be fine looking people. I loved them all, as much as I was allowed to, cause they all went to the community shack to be raised. But Always was, somehow, my favorite. I guess because she was the first thing mine, after my mother. I always sneaked by the community shack and took her into my little shack with me. I knew mostly the nights the Young Master was comin, and when I made a mistake and he came when I didn't expect him, it was like that child was grown.

She would lay under that bed and not make a sound. Sometimes, when he left, she would be sleep with her thumb in her mouth like I used to be. I'd gently haul her out and into my arms and rock us both back to sleep. But that didn't happen too often cause the Young Master had plenty women on that farm to take hisself, and did. He was his best machine on that farm cause he made many a baby to sell. I could see Always was goin to be a sure-nuff pretty girl and she had such sweet ways. Sweet ways. Oh that child was sweet! Heart just full of love. She loved everything. Trees, flowers, cats, dogs, cows, pigs, horses, rocks, people, babies, everything! She would share any and everything she had! Even beg you to share yours with somebody else! I worried about her heart so full of love, would it be able to stand what I knew was in store. I thought I knew what her life was going to be even before she lived it. So I loved her hard as I could, much as I could, and kept her stomach full of all the good food I could steal, beg, or borrow. I knew the day would come when I, like my mama, would not be able to help her . . . so I did all I could do while I could do it. Even so, there was times she was struck near dumb and left with ugly bruises from the Mistress's hands. I could only hold her and kiss them cruel marks when I came in from the fields. I would think, hard, of runnin away with all my children. But then . . . I would look out crost the world far as I could see and I didn't know nothin bout what was out there or whichever way freedom might be. I thought white folks was everywhere and owned everything on earth.

Yes, I heard the rumors runnin round bout some of the white people who did not like us to be slaves . . . but you know we wasn't gonna blive that! Believe some of these same kinda people who took everything we had from us, beat us half to death sometimes, hated us all the time . . . was gonna set us free? White folks? You'd a had to be fool crazy to blive somethin like that! More rumors was round said some slaves had run and made it. Made it to Freedom! Not no slave nomore! I wondered where they ran to . . . cause the Masters had told us how them people out there in the North thought slave meat was good for eatin and ate em! And that way, way off, far off up more North, they hated slaves with any color to they skin . . . and killed them right off, first sight they had of em! So I wondered where them who had made it to freedom had run off to. Sometime I would just stand, squeezin my eyes at the stars in the sky and try to guess which way was North or whatever way freedom was. But the sky is so big and endless, like time. I couldn't make nothin of it. I couldn't run off anyway. My children was too small and I couldn't leave em. Couldn't! Sometimes I'd think, if I could read, I could help all of us. I'd be in the house, cleaning, and I be dustin those books and I would slip one out with me when I'd leave, knowin I be beat most to death if I'm caught with it, but sometime you just don't give a damn no more when you tryin to learn how to live some other kind of life. And I thought the answer might be in all them crooked marks on that white paper. I couldn't tell nobody I got it. Nobody! All I could do is sit in the out-house or that chicken house and stare at that book. Turn it one side up then the other. I finally buried one in the ground in that chicken house to save for Always. Maybe we could learn it together.

I needed help . . . and there was none. None. But still, ever once in a while I'd go dig up my book and stare into it some more, then bury it again. I now know the name of that book. One thing really made me think. And made me want to read so bad. Was a new man slave brought here in chains. He was caught talkin and even readin somethin to the other slaves in a shack one night. That man they called boy was beat with that whip til he was gone dead cause he kept laughin tween his screams of pain. The beater had to even stop and rest! The beater was tired! You know how they musta beat that man! But he kept laughin tween his screams sayin, "I can READ! And the Lord God HATES you for what you is doin to my people." Then he laugh again. Say, "I can

READ!" He screamed them words til he couldn't scream no more, then he mumbled them into the ground, into his own blood, mucus, and tears. That's how he died. Them was his last words on earth. "I can read. The truth has set me free and I know you ain't nothin, white man. The Lord ain't give us to you." SLASH! WHOSH! SLASH! went that whip again.

But he was most gone, couldn't hardly hear him then, but he said it one more time: "I can read." Then he died. The Master bade them keep whippin him even if he was dead. Ain't that somethin sad? And still, that wasn't the meanest thing I ever seen done on that place was my home. Home. All I could do for myself and my children was to add a stone to my little collection-horde every year to keep our ages clear. That was mine. That was us. Nobody knew bout it . . . so they couldn't take it away. I couldn't count in a real way but I knew I had a rock for every year for everybody in my real family. Not my slave brothers and sisters, but my little children I birthed. My family.

One day when the family was bout to have some special party I was called in the house to do some extra cleaning. I was doin my work but I had my last baby on my hip. I could still do my work good cause I was used to workin holdin a child. See . . . in the fields where they make you lay your baby down over to the side while you work three or four hours fore you come back to see bout that baby? Well, some of them babies have died from sunstroke, or snakebite or be eatin up a bit by somethin that was hungry. I learned to hide my baby in my sack or tote it on my back or carry it in my arm. I had trained myself to work good like that so the seer wouldn't stop me from doin it.

Anyway, the Young Mistress come in and was lookin at my baby who was lookin like her husband. I just kept workin. Then that Mistress leaped at me and commenced to slappin me with her hands, first, then a poker that was kept by the fireplace. She hit my baby, oh Lord. Now, I could take a beatin from her. But I was holdin my baby and my baby was too young to take a beatin. Well . . . I took that poker away from her!! We was both of us shocked! I was shocked to be a fool to struggle with the Mistress of my life, and she was shocked at the sudden change in our way-situation roles, and we was like stuck in time, just starin at each other. Her arm raised to strike and the poker raised in my hand to strike her back! Now! We stood there like we was stone, lookin hard in each other's eyes and from somewhere the idea came that this woman who was built like me, shaped like me, had eyes, nose, ears, arms, legs, and blood just like me didn't know what she was doin in this here thing either. The Master of the Land was Master of us both, and all of us, in this thing and she was captured in a net just like I, as a slave, in this net of time. But . . . she loved him, the Master, while I did not. She had her pain alright, but, I knew mine was worser cause I had her kind of pain . . . and my own and my children's too. AND he liked her, which made her life better. He didn't care a damn for me . . . I was nothin, and nothin I had for him was nothin either. She should have helped me . . . not struck me for bein a slave to him. I would have helped her. Our eyes had stared so hard they had to blink.

We blinked. I put the poker back and left, holdin my baby who I had made safe . . . for a time. I was sposed to be helpin to bake in the kitchen then, but I went to that old broke-down chicken house again and cried over my baby. Another girl, white as her daddy, headin for trouble all her life. No, I was wrong, she wasn't headin for trouble, she was already in it! Then, after while, I commenced to thinkin bout my mother who had killed herself. I thought and I thought. After another little while, I quit cryin and went out with my baby in my arm, gatherin every kind of poison weed I knew and some I didn't know. I started cryin again thinkin bout what I was plannin to do to my children. Tears and snot mingled together with the blood from the scratches in my hands, but I kept pickin. Wouldn't change my mind. Couldn't.

I looked out over them beautiful fields, up into that beautiful sky so full of soft white clouds and the sun so warm and good to shine down on this earth. I saw them tall beautiful trees, weavin and wavin in the winds that come from all crost the earth. I saw birds. Birds what was free to fly off or stay, whatever they wanted . . . free. Better off than me and my slave sisters and brothers. Even the snakes and bugs at my feet was free. That little mosquito was free. But not me. I was cryin when I told God he don't need to give me everything . . . just mercy. Just a little mercy. That would be kind enough. I didn't see no change in store for me tho. And I knew soon as that white Mistress reported that I had raised my hand with that poker at her I would be tied down and beat to the very end of my life.

My babies would see that. They would have no more mother, worthless even as she was to them, they needed me for whatever I could do for em, if it wasn't nothin but to steal food to fill their bellies. I built me a fire and boiled them poison weeds, made a kind of dinner. Then I went and got my children from all round where they were, most at poor old Miz Elliz's. I kissed Miz Elliz, surprised her, cause she didn't know what I was gettin ready to do. Kissed her good-by, but didn't say it, cause she the only person I could think of almost like a piece of family. I took my children, my beautiful children, served their tinplates and fed them.

It was a little bitter, yet I forced them to eat. I

really meant for Always to die right beside me cause she was the oldest and I knew her hard times was right on her for soon. Then we all layed down. I knew we was dyin, they didn't. But they lay down like I told them . . . and slept. Do you know what happened?! I died. But my children who I was tryin to save . . . lived. Some kind of way they only got sick. Oh very sick, but not dead! I died and left them children and Always in that terrible world, in these bitter times, all alone. Now, I was dead but I could feel my heart still grievin. My soul was not at rest! Was it cause my children was left behind me? Oh Lord!

Now, I'm gonna tell you somethin I don't understand, not even to this day and this is many, many years later. I know now when people die they lay down in their graves til the resurrection. But before I got to my grave, I grieved and cried and screamed, beggin for my children bein all alone. Beggin God to let me stay with them. But my body layin dead on that cornshuck bed never moved a lick. It was too late. I was dead. Somehow, I didn't go nowhere. I saw them find my body, I heard what everybody said. I didn't really have to listen cause it seemed I knew what all was in everybodies' mind before they spoke out. I watched them dump my body in a tight little grave off in some dumpy ground in the slave cemetery. Watched them cover it up. Watched my babies cryin for their mama. Watched em bein slapped by old Mistress for makin all that noise. Watched em hold back their tears. I was watchin cause I wasn't in with my body. I was at a distance, yet I was close.

Now God didn't say nothin to me. Wasn't no angel sent down to tell me nothin bout what was happenin to me. The devil didn't say nothin either, thank God. I was just left. Just out there in nothin, bein nothin. Some way tho, I knew why I was bein left out. I coulda cried for joy but I didn't know how to, with my new self I had. I blive I was left out here so I could watch over my children, my blood, my Always . . . just for a little while. That is why I am able to tell you this now. "They" forgot about me for many years of Time. I have seen many, many things. Saw Times change, saw Times stay the same. I understood, at last, many things with a new kind of sense. I could almost read all minds. I did read many minds many times. Mankind is not so complex as he is foolish. That's what makes things complicated for them.

I found out if I had waited, lived, somehow, twenty more years I would have been set free at the end of that war. Times wasn't much better from the ground up, but we was then free to suffer on our own . . . for our own, by our own, from our own, to our own. Free. I shoulda waited. Anyway . . . the most important thing was I was able to watch my children. But I mostly watched Always. First I must tell you somethin tho. This dead-but-not-gone thing was not like being a ghost, I don't think. I seem to know all kinds of different knowledge floatin round in space. I couldn't touch nothin, but I could think . . . and I could move.

i have to be careful bout goin off to sleep tho, cause once I dozed off by side of a ocean, it was so peaceful, so beautiful, such a marvelous work of God, I just lay my soul down by a tree whose shape was all wild like the oceans. I fell asleep . . . and when I woke up it was sixty years later! It went by quick as a minute! Look what I musta missed! Time is different wherever I am, not like it is on earth. No wonder God moves in his own time . . . it's not the same as we know it. I'll tell you somethin else, too.

The sky is round as the earth! Only bigger, larger, huge, ever so huge that it holds many planets and things. That's why it is endless. It's round.

CHAPTER 4

I HAD NAMED my children, Always, which you know, then came Sun. He was my son so I named him Sun. Then came Peach, then Plum. I don't know what all they put in the books on my babies, but them was the names I gave em. The Young Mistress named her children, Loretta and Virginia. All my children were sad because I was gone, but Always took it the hardest. She had been closest to me with the time we spent together.

My heart grieved for all of em. But they was

young and they sure was kept busy as slaves. Always was twelve years old, Sun was eleven, Peach, ten, Plum, one year old. The big house kept Always busier than ever. At twelve years old she took up most of my jobs and kept all her own and when it came time for her to be restin, that Ole Mistress found somethin else for her to do and slapped, pinched, pulled her hair and, oh, did all them little nasty things cruel old folks can find to do to somebody helpless. Was always a bruise or two on my baby's face and body.

The Young Mistress didn't want Always in the house cause she was too pretty. Prettier than her own children and looked as much as a girl can look like her father and still be pretty. But, Ole Mistress didn't pay the young one no mind, so when one Mistress wasn't slappin Always for one thing, the other Mistress slapped her for another. She got it both ways.

Always didn't know she was pretty. It's somethin you may not know, but most slaves that ain't in the house in a regular job, never see a mirror. Never get to see what they look like. Ain't that somethin? Can live all your life and never know what your own face looks like! Can look in water, but then your face be movin in waves, can't see it good and clear.

Always just pull her hair back and plait it, throw water on her face, and go to work in the dark part of the mornin. But, bein in that big house so much she got to see herself and it came to her that she was white. Most white as her mistresses. Always got mad and stayed mad from then on.

I watched and wished I was there to talk to her, splain to her some parts bout life I knew, but I couldn't. So her little mind just had to struggle and strain to try to understand this thing called life she was livin. Miz Elliz tried to mother my children for me to cover their loss. But she was old and tired too, and had nine or ten others to worry bout. Sides, slaves was used to someone dear and close that they loved bein taken away. Just natural.

They always expected, feared it, even in the face of the Master's promises that turned false mostly every time. She did teach them manners tho and tried to tell them ways to stay 'way from white folks trouble. See . . . my son was all time talkin bout runnin away, that scared the old woman cause she knew it might end the life of all my children whether he got way safe or not.

Cause they would spect him to come back for em or that they would try to follow their brother. If they caught him . . . Lord, Lord. Ohhh, don't most people in the world, even today, know what they did to a man tryin to run to freedom when they got their hands and guns, whips and knives and boards on him!? I prayed he would wait. He was so young, so weak in compare to them, so ignorant of the woods and rivers.

There was more and more talk bout a war comin and freedom. The slaves didn't get no straight-out clear information, but the words was in the air. Just couldn't connect em to mean much to a life that didn't know nothin else but what it had already seen and lived. I could see it acoming from where I was lookin, but I couldn't tell nobody. Couldn't tell my slave sisters and brothers. Couldn't tell my son. To wait. Just a little longer.

Sides, I didn't have his exact feelins . . . and he was sufferin from that Young Mistress. She had done forgot that day in her house when she saw I was human as she was. Or maybe she didn't forget, just had to keep provin it wasn't true that we was human like her. Cause she found the hardest and dirtiest things for Sun to do. I could only watch. Oh, do you know a mother's heart?

I noticed while I was watchin tho, that the oldest daughter, Loretta, watched my son whenever she was near where he was. I knew her mind. I saw she was knowin he was her half-brother . . . and thank God, she was sorry for him.

Isn't it strange, how people can have hearts that look alike, but have all different things in em? I mean, they have said all people can love, and I'm not sure I blive that. Seems like some people have only a drop of love in their hearts and they even have a hard time lovin themselves cause that drop dries up with instructions from their mind or maybe just not usin it. Then some people have so much love in their hearts that they don't have a hard time lovin people and things they don't even know. Then you got all them that's in the middle of them two. And some, I blive, with no love at all in em. The way they lives proves it!

Loretta was kind in her heart. She was only bout twelve years old. One day she brought him some cake to the backyard where he was turnin the ground for the house garden. She sat down on a little bench out there, he didn't look at her direct but he did know she was there. She sat a bit, then got up and laid the cake down by his tools, said, "This is for you." He just kept on aworkin til he worked on over there where his tools and that cake was, then taken it up and worked with one hand hoein the weeds and eatin that cake, shovin it in his mouth fore somebody saw it. Mumblin "thankee."

She sat kickin the dirt neath her feet. Then she ask him, "What you think bout your life here?" Well, he didn't know much about life, but he knew enough to say, "I wants a life like yours." She say, "I don't see as how you can get it cause they calls you a negro-nigger, cause your mammy was a nigger-woman."

Crumbs fallin down his chin, he say, "My mama wasn't no mammy. She was my motha." I smiled in my heart.

She say, "Well everybody knows that's what you call em, is mammy."

My Sun say, "No mam, that what white folks call em. We call our mother, mama . . . when she was livin."

She say, "Well, anyway, you ain't really a white boy, all white boy. You got nigga blood in you."

He wiped his face with the sleeve of his raggedy little shirt, hit a hard lick with that hoe. "I knows it."

After she look around, she ask, "You think you gonna run away?" I got no need to breathe, but I gasped then.

He got wary. "Naw . . . I don't think so. Ain't never thought on it." I knew he thought of it everyday.

Now this Loretta wasn't smilin nor laughin through none of this talkin they was doin. She was a serious child. She asked him, "Cause you don't know how?"

Sun hit at a mosquito or two, kicked a small rock out the way with his bare foot, said, "I betta get on back to my work," as he turned back to his job. They both looked thoughtful.

Now Young Mistress had been watchin from

the kitchen windows. She snatched the door open and hollered, "Boy! Get back to your work! You lazy!"

Loretta looked at her mother with a mixture of annoyance and fear, then got up and walked slowly cross the yard and up the steps through the door her mother was holdin open for her.

Somethin musta just been in that child that day cause she spoke in a low hard voice to her mama, "Don't you dare call him nigger. He is our half-brother." And the Young Mistress sent her flyin cross that room with a slap so hard I almost felt it!

Young Mistress say, "No child what ain't come from my body is no kin to you! That nigga-boy ain't nothin to you! He ain't nothin but a picaninny nigga is what he is! And all of em! You ain't got no brother til I give you one! You heah?"

And so that passed, but Sun wasn't lowed to work that particular piece of land nomore, so close to the house. Howsomever, them children did find ways to talk again. Out back of one of the barns or near the new chicken house, wherever he was workin. Loretta always brought him some fruit or somethin, always had a gift in her hands for him. They just made small-talk mongst the manure and the weeds, with the cows lowin and hens just apeckin round.

Then, one day, she asked him, "What kind of present would you like to have that you would keep forever?"

He stop workin and leaned on the rake. He trusted her more now. After a moment he looked round carefully, lowered his voice, said, "I wants to read."

Her eyes got so big and round, "My daddy would even beat me to pieces if I helped you learn to read."

He lifted the rake and slowly went back to work. But he knew her now cause they been pretty close talkin for bout a year. Still, fore she left, she said, "You know it's gainst the laws for niggers to learn to read!"

He stopped workin again, looked at her a moment, said, "But you done tol me I ain't no purdee nigga. And I ain't! Look!" He held his arm out. "I am mos white as you. Your daddy is my pappy."

For some reason the little girl, Loretta, burst into tears and ran from the place. Too young and confused, if I guess right. It musta hurt her bout her daddy, too. She knew it, but nobody ever done said it.

The day did come, soon, when she would take to doin her lessons in the shady backyard. Then, soon, she was wanderin off to the woods. In them days everybody had woods. Big, huge, tall shady trees, all kinds, but mostly pines. Sun would meet her out there and she would teach him bout readin and numbers and things. Three years passed like that. He would transfer his information, without a book, to Always and Peach, while Plum, too young, just set listenin.

Them children had to be mighty careful and they knew it, was raised knowin it. Even round other slaves, cause even a slave would tell on another slave. Some folks will do somethin for somebody they know don't like them no kinda way, for a moment's empty attention, which doins only gets them known in the big house as a "good nigga" to the white folks. Yet, them white folks really didn't respect you for tellin on your own kind. Thought you was nothin in their hearts. That's why so many of em thought we was ignorant fools to the bone.

Anyway, my children learned. They still had their own personal jar of pebbles for their age, but Sun showed em how to count to twenty, far as he could go and not get confused, then they didn't need them pebbles nomore. In these things the pain of losin me and bein, in a way, alone, was forgotten.

Peach was Sun's favorite, cause Always seem to be mean and serious all the time. Peach was womanish, dainty and delicate. She envied Loretta her clothes and nice bedroom as she lay on her cornshucks and pulled her raggedy sackcloth shirtdress close round her little cold body. As she would fall asleep nights, she would lay there thinkin of ways to get into the big house to work, where them pretty things was and them mirrors.

Peach finally got Sun to ask Loretta to let her be her personal slave to keep up her room. That took a couple of months cause Young Mistress did not want my children in her house that close and that clean, as Peach would have to be. That was too close to bein human. And, Virginia, who was a very plump girl, with acne, stringy hair and stingy ways, hated slaves. She hated slaves cause that was the only thing worse off than her, that she could be better than. And a pretty nigga-slave was a bomination to her. When Virginia said her prayers to God even, she prayed that Peach and every other pretty lookin slave would die. She fully expected God to mind her. And she wanted to be the one to whip some of them to death with that whip that hung in the storage shack which she liked to play with.

Howsomever it went, Loretta was a strong one and she knew to ask her daddy more often than her mother, and Peach got her job-place in the house.

Now Peach was not my hardest workin child. She was extra lazy. But because there was so much extra comin to her from this job; the touch of the clothes, the feel of a carpet neath her wide, bare feet, smells of the scents on dressers, the mirrors, Peach kept Loretta's clothes neat, clean, washed, ironed, and hung up in the closet. The room was kept spic and span. The dresser dusted, oiled, shined, drawers lined. She never needed scoldin.

Peach slept on the floor at the foot of the bed. Loretta let her, even with her kind heart. See . . . sometimes you can think you are bein too good and Loretta needed to know she was the Mistress. Needed Peach to remember it. Cause sometimes when they played games together, Peach forgot and commanded Loretta to do things. There wasn't nothin better that could get Loretta to remember Peach was, after all, a nigger, than to hear a command from Peach's too full lips. Then too, Virginia might be round some corner or behind some curtain, watchin and listenin.

I watched and I saw my Peach was learning things to help her in her future, I thought, I hoped. I could see, if freedom came in time, before they sold her out to one of them sick-minded white men who does cruel things to women . . . she could be alright.

See . . . I could see some things in the future, but I could not see everything. God is the only One Who sees everything. I knew Sun would be alright in lookin out for hisself if he could just keep takin in knowledge without nobody findin out. I hoped that knowledge wouldn't make him no fool to speak up out of turn and cause him to lose his life. And Peach's life. And Plum's life. And my Always.

Now, it may seem as tho these children was doin alright and that bein slaves wasn't hard to them cause they was makin some kind of way. But it is so hard to explain to anybody how each minute, each hour, each day had to be lived. Yes, you was fed, and clothed of a sort, you had a place to sleep. But count your own life and see, even with these important things taken care of, how much more there is to life. Would you exchange freedom for these small things given to you? No . . . not given . . . well paid for. If each minute could be your last even in this little measly way, if the next hour you could blong to somebody you ain't never seen nor heard of . . . somebody more cruel, fierce, tricky, unfeelin, who really did think you was a animal and showed it with every move and word they did and said.

Now . . . I will tell you what I have seen and

noticed in life from where I am. There ain't no two people, or very few, that you can put together and they be happy, even if they think each other is equals. Mothers, fathers, children, and every human bein on God's earth have to work hard at gettin along with each other. Now just spose they didn't feel like workin at it? Ain't no two people who work a job together can get along more'n two days without one of them thinkin bad thoughts bout the other. Don't care what color they are. People is human. You hear what I'm tellin you! Now put you on your job with your boss and give them all license to treat you just any way they want to . . . You see what I mean? The courts is full and will always be full of people and the grievances they put on each other til the end of our time.

Well . . . a slave didn't have no court to go to. The Masters of the Land made the law . . . so the law could not hurt them. I bet you couldn't live like a slave one hour even in a game. Well, my children was strugglin for survival in the day of no-win. Only slave. It was no game, it was their lives.

The day did come when Sun ran away. I followed him. That Loretta girl had give him some money she had been savin the hard way, cause the farm was not so prosperous now, the Master runnin round, and drinkin, cause he thought HE was unhappy at home. His home. Sun was most fifteen years old then, Loretta was sixteen. He passed for white and, in the end, it got good to him and he never passed back to his own mother's color again. But, I done gone too far ahead of my story.

As all these other things was goin on, there was Always. Always was what you might call mean with responsibility. My daughter had tried to take my place in lookin after her brother and sisters. She scolded and fought them bout things they did, for their own safety. She was always tryin to keep Plum in hand, close to her.

Miz Elliz had asked for her to help in the child-keepin, so that was the work she did half the time. So she could be round her own family, you see? They let her, but that Ole Mistress said she was too young and strong to be just doin that kind of work, so she still had to do ALL her other duties at the same time. Her hard work grew so sometimes that chile only got two or three hours sleep a night.

I watched my children, always prayin, to keep them from the beatins, punishments, hunger, grief and misery that is soul and core of the life of a slave. To see my, or any child workin, slavin in that hot, heavy sun that falls on your life like a big ole weight.

Diggin in ground hard and full of weeds, snakes, and scorpions. To pull and drag things that strip the hands of flesh, make them to bleed. To never look up and say "Tomorrow . . . I can rest. This evenin, I can rest." To bury hands to the shoulders in hot water boiling over a fire, filled with lye soap, to wash another person's dirt, for no pay and no thanks. To cook and serve, sick or well, serve people that don't care how you feel, never think of what is in your mind, in your heart. Them white people made hate. They made hate just like they had a formula for it and followed that formula down to the last exact gallon of misery put in. Well . . . that's what they made and that's what they got.

I'm tell you this. There was still some, a few,

of them real niggas that loved them white folks! Loved them. Was proud of any job they had that would make them close to the Master. That they looked down on another slave just like them, as if they, themselves, was better cause they was close to the Master of all this misery. It's some folks out there, in your world, right now, today, are like that. All colors. Watch them . . . cause they are fools. To kiss the hand with the whip in it . . . and scorn the hand of friendship with somebody like yourself . . . is a sign of insanity . . . to me. Now, I ain't sayin be no fool. . . . What I am sayin is . . . don't be no fool.

Now other people ain't no fool all the time either. Young Mistress noticed that Sun didn't walk and work like he had no hope, like he was in some misery all the time now. She watched Loretta closer. Natural it come up, in time, that Sun was goin to be sold. Sides that, things wasn't goin too well on that farm. Land dryin up, wearin out. Slaves gettin old. So many cost so much to keep up. The talk of war which was sittin right on the tail of the South made slaves hard to deal with at that time. And people, white people didn't take to slaves what was too light round there. Had to go down to New Orleans if you wanted to sell them.

Old Mistress was fussin and carryin on bout all the money the farm was losin with no good care, even while she ate her pecan fudgies, baked ham and chicken and rich stuffs. But it didn't do no good with her son. She was so big and fat now, she didn't hardly come out the house so she couldn't see everything. But she knew there was sposed to be money out there in them fields and in them niggers.

What Old Mistress didn't know was her son had picked up a dis-ease on one of them trips to somewhere tryin to sell some of the slaves. He had passed it round to some of his own women slaves at home. Them slaves didn't know when they had nothin . . . so wasn't nobody tryin to cure nobody. So sides all the money bein lost, other things—meanin money—was bein lost too! Oh, things was really goin down.

That's when the special trip was planned for to go to New Orleans to sell more slaves, more human hearts. Loretta knew Sun was goin to go if he stayed there til the coffle left. As time had passed she felt of him more like a brother. I don't know why, or what was really in her heart, cause she didn't pay no mind to my other children too much, sides Peach, and that's cause Peach worked good for her.

Loretta gathered money, much as she could squeeze and "borrow" out of her mama and grandmother. That chile took some of her father's best clothes and a satchel. She got, someway lyin, Sun to carry her to the town in that carriage her mama had begged for and got. She bought Sun his ticket, helped him dress, and put him on a boat. She waved her hankerchief good-by to her "brother." He promised he would write and let her know everything, using the name "Mr. Freer." Wasn't they just children?

But her daddy, his daddy, had him taken off at the very next stop. Somebody had seen and told. Probably somebody was a slave. Maybe not.

Anyway, Loretta got excused with a scoldin cause "that nigga had fooled her with his lyin tongue." Sun got a hundred lashes with a whip what had metal tips on it. Got rubbed down with salty brine and cayenne pepper. Got chained to the plow, night and day, to pull right on long with the mule. Ate only bread and water for thirty days. Hadn't been for Always sneakin him out some fruit Loretta had given her, now and then, that boy woulda died. Oh, and the care and medicine she put on him at night when she should have been restin from her work. She would fuss with him, then cry with him and hug him and call my name, "Mama . . . mama."

When he came off that, almost dead, Ole Mistress said he needed cleanin out from all them runnin ideas. She gave him a dose of castor oil and more cayenne pepper to clean his insides out. They almost tore my boy's insides out! Oh God, oh, God. How he made it, I do not know. I really do not know.

Three months after that, they tried again, Sun and Loretta. Only this time they darken his skin with somethin and he "passed" for Black. They wrapped his better clothes and things up in a large neat package and she told the train conductor he was takin a package to her brother in a city, was headin up North, and that her brother would meet

him and send ole Joe back, "to be sure and see
that ole Joe got there alright."

Ole Joe was bent over, couldn't hardly talk and
just set all the way with his hat pull down mos
over his face, sleepin. Sun's last words to Loretta
was that he would write soon as he saw "Mr.
Freer," and to take care of Peach. He didn't say
"all" his sisters cause I guess he didn't want to
weigh too heavy on the little lady who was helpin
him to freedom. He knew Loretta didn't like Peach
so much cause he did love her. Well, sometime
jealousy gets in even a kind heart.

I don't need to tell you what all went on when
they found that Sun was gone, this time for good.
They advertised, they sent patrollers, they did all
what they could with as little money as they could.
They almos rather spend money tho, then have a
slave out-do em. They watched Loretta, but she
was so mean, slappin and carryin on with Peach,
they stopped suspectin her havin anything to do
with it this second time. Peach caught hell.

Bout six months later Sun's first letter came.
Said it was from "Reverend" and they knew Sun

couldn't write, so nobody paid no mind to it, don't ask me why. He spoke so much bout how Peach could join him and he could take care of her til she found work and all like that, didn't say nothin bout Loretta, cept thanks.

It's the strangest things come outta life sometime. Loretta got her mama to get her daddy to sell Peach. My baby Peach! Peach was sold. Wasn't hard cause she was pretty and with the good food from the big house, she had a well-formed body, even bein so young.

A man from somewhere cross the waters bought her, was rich. Now I can make this short. Peach was not no fool. She had fooled round in that big house and read them few books they had, much as she could. She had read somethin bout them Rabian Nights what had told her somethin bout men and women. Peach was scared, didn't know nothin bout life but from that farm and them few books Loretta lowed her to read. But Peach worked on that man. He bought her nice things to wear and she looked good in em, so he bought her nicer things, beautiful things. She could cook, set a table, speak sweet and soft, and be quiet when she didn't know what she and anybody else was talkin bout.

Now, the man had had a wife was a little older than him when he bought Peach. Don't know why, maybe it was natural, but that wife didn't live much more than seven or eight months from the time he brought Peach home. That man took Peach and moved back to Scotland or somewhere over there and . . . married her! Married my Peach.

I was tryin to watch my children, my blood, but it was gettin all spread out. Now some of my black blood was in Scotland somewhere. I understand tho, I understand. Peach used the only things she had to work with to escape the life of a slave. She changed her name to Peachel and pronounced it Pe-SHEL.

Now. I had wanted to stay round and watch my family blood, see my family grow, if it could survive slavery. And it was growin. But it was growin in so many different lands and colors. I wouldn'ta recognized my own children's children, my own blood, if I hadda met them comin down the street right in front of my face.

Years later, when Peach's, well, Peachel's grandchildren was all round her and some were darker than the others, they ask her "Why?" That ole Peach just laughed and told em, "Cause I'm from America! We are all colors in America! And you are American because I am!" She never told the whole truth, but she never really tried to hide it or was fraid of it either. "Your grandmother, my mother, would have loved you." That's all she ever told them bout me.

Being rich, their children, Peach's and her husband, went to college. Became things like doctors, lawyers, judges, and married doctors, lawyers, judges. Even into royalty. My blood ran like it was let loose from a stream into the river, into the ocean. It ran. It ran from the French wife Sun married, through his four children to theirs. Ran into the world, hidden, but THERE. But, I am ahead of my story again.

CHAPTER 5

ALWAYS WAS LEFT with Plum, still slaves on the land. The land where the Master of the Land was destroyin the land . . . and the slaves and his pitiful little wife. I returned in time to see them buryin Ole Mistress. She died from sugar diabetes, high blood pressure, heart trouble, and somethin they now call hypertension.

The farm had fallen down so quick, in such a short time, til I hadn't realized how far down they had gone til I saw the funeral for Ole Mistress. It was a shabby one. Not at all like the one she musta dreamed of.

Young Master had the coffin built right in the yard, front of the house by the slave carpenters. Didn't get no fancy one from the town and didn't send out no notices. Them people was maybe not comin anyway. Cause they was worried.

Sons talkin bout a war to preserve their way of life so they could keep destroyin the lives of slaves. Well, that's what it was. Most of their land had done given out, just used up. And slaves was runnin off . . . and gettin away! Some masters was in debt. Deep debt. The rumors and wars was turnin things all up and round.

I don't really know it all cause I wasn't in their business so much, I just noticed all that in a glance at life. With the farm doin so poorly, all slaves what wasn't more raggedy, was dirty and mos let to stay that way. Food was low. Young Mistress was grievin, tired and exhausted tryin to keep up a tradition of superiority. Takes money to do that and money was surely low and slow. I blive it was round 1844 or so.

The Young Master was dyin from his dis-ease,

really body-old. His long yellow fingernails only plucked at the few pretty, thin slaves he had round there on that ole farm. Some of em even his daughters.

When he wanted favors from a slave now, since the slave knew he couldn't complain on em, they made him pay some little somethin, some little favor in return for a feel. Shame to be said, but a small coin here, a small pretty thing there, counts! Specially when you ain't got nothin. Them slaves wasn't happy bout it, but when you ain't got nothin . . . and don't see nothin comin . . . See? A starvin man will eat dirty bread.

Someway Always had missed the disease. Too tired. Too busy. Not wantin none of them ole men left on the farm. I reckon she had some of her ancestors' blood runnin through her mind. She was raggedy, but she was clean and still pretty in a thin kind of way. Plum was bout five years old now. My daughters stayed close to each other, workin most times.

Plum was a bit kinda sickly. Delicate. Nothin Always nor Miz Elliz could put a finger on, but somethin was there. The child had no appetite, didn't eat hardly nothin. So she was extra dear to Always cause the link with her family was only gonna be as strong as Plum was. Sometime love is a hard thing to make in them kinda circumstances my children lived in, but they made a love and it held them together and probly kept em from goin crazy. I know Plum loved Always so much, she didn't even–not always tell her when she was in pain. Just go off in some corner of that old chicken house, hide her face in her arms and suck her thumb til she could feel better. Such a little tyke . . . all alone. My heart yearned to be in that chicken house with her . . . to hold her, comfort her, make her well. I couldn't. Then the time showed up to sell some of the last slaves, to keep the big house goin.

One of the men who showed up, Doak Butler, didn't live too far away. Maybe eighteen miles or so. In his life his mama and papa had only had two slaves. The man slave died from overwork.

One woman, old but still livin, took care his sick brother, Jason. The brother was sick cause he had got struck down one day, sawin trees. Got hit. Had just ruined his spine, wasted his legs. His mind was mostly alright but he couldn't talk clear, couldn't walk.

This young man, Doak, was getting married. He wanted to make a showin and needed a slave for his young wife-to-be. To show he was some kind of class gentry. He already had a little land. He, this man, looked upon my daughter, Always. And he was pleased. I liked to died, again. And . . . he couldn't afford my little Plum. Ohhh! Tear my heart up, life. Just tear my heart up! You done always done it! Just keep on, keep on . . . til I can't even stand death.

Doak was gettin married to what he considered a genteel lady name Wanda Sue, but called "Sue." In truth she was a hard-workin young woman, Christian upbringin, shy, reserved, delicate constitution as the times called for, about to be what came early in those days, a old maid. She did believe she was superior to the darker race cause it had been bred in her, but she was not cruel. She was a virgin and willin to do her duty by her husband and give him sons as her father and mother told her to do. She wasn't so glad to get Doak but she was glad to get a husband and her own home.

As far as genteel ancestors, hers was like most of everybodies'. A female ancestor had been sent to America as a white bondswoman and served her seven years in hard work. Course, whatever she had done to get them seven years, poverty had done made her do it. She got to America and times was just as hard here, but more opportunity to work in a clean, growin land. And course she knew she would be free someday. In her years here, need turned to opportunity and a good solid marriage with a hard-workin man. Their family grew, always workin hard. They had a few slaves, worked them hard. Then some kinda trouble hit em hard and they lost a lot, long with the right to choose a better, more prosperous husband for Sue. She was now, like I said, goin to marry Doak and he was gettin a slave for her to show he was quality folks. And, like I said, he saw Always.

Doak also saw Loretta. For Loretta, the times was harder and men were few. But, bein like she was, she kept herself a distance from all what she thought to be beneath her, like poor white trash. It never seem to touch her that her family was gettin poorer and the farm in debt. Course, she wasn't trash. She was well bred, got to give her mama that. She wanted her girls to be ladies, and one was.

Loretta was also lookin more to hear from Sun. Not from lovin him as a man, I don't think, but just to hope he found a way to get wealthy and send for her, pay her back and get her away from the empty country life she was livin. She dreamed of having beautiful things again and bein a beautiful woman too. Just like life, everybody dreamin.

Virginia saw him . . . and felt she had fallen in love as far as her hard little narrow heart would let her. She peeped through windows, peeped behind curtains, looked round corners, and found a hundred excuses to come through the front parlor when her mama and Doak was talkin business. Young Mistress had taken over tryin to run the farm, tryin to stay on top of hard times and life.

When he told Young Mistress he wanted a maid-servant for his future bride, "I am to be wed in the very short future. I wanted to buy . . .

purchase the nigga woman in time to train her a bit fore my bride comes in to home."

Mistress looked him over very carefully. She had two daughters, marriageable age. No suitor in sight cept some Reverend who had been writing Loretta for too long a time not to asaid somethin besides Praise Jesus, as Loretta reported he said. And this here man may not be rich but he was landed and had money enough to buy a slave, where THEY had to sell one!

She bowed her head, folded the money, and placin it discreetly in a drawer, said, "Well suh! I surely hope everything goes well for you all. We may be havin a weddin someday soon ourselves. My two lovely daughters, you know."

He bowed his head and smiled as a southern gentleman would. "Yes mam, I seen em. They be right lovely beautiful young ladies."

Young Mistress stood as she said, "They have so many suitors, they just haven't decided which to choose. But if I had known such a handsome and worthy gentleman was just down the road from us, we would have included you in some of our functions here at SwallowLand."

Doak perked up. Thought, "Oh! I am a gentle-man! It showed, did it?" He brightened, thinkin of Loretta momentarily. "Yes mam!"

Young Mistress called a house slave, old Dora, and sent her for Always, and ordered lemonade for Doak. All the slaves knew somebody was goin that day. They'd been goin so reglar. One or two when different kinds of white men try to look them over.

The mood, the atmosphere of the slave quarters was sad and gray and blue. Deep sighs, hand clasps, tender touches, tired walks off a space or so, then a return to sit and handle old belongins what wasn't nothin but just dear to someone who ain't had nothin else.

The house what wasn't never their home was now home in a different way. The real old ones, or sick ones was only a little better off, cause some-time they would be gotten rid of. They was only takin up space and food sorely needed now and they couldn't work as hard for their upkeep. Slave dealers can do a whoppin lot to a old slave to spruce him up for a week or so. Til they gray hair start showin again and the shiny grease wears off.

These old ones loved each other, most of em, as family. And you know it don't feel good, not knowin where you goin and who you goin to and if you can make a new family feelin without the time to give it. And this old work may be hard, but the beatins was fewer now, cept for that Virginia when she had stole some liquor and drinked it and come out afta em to "play." So . . . all of em was nervous and scared. Even the animals acted like they felt it. Even some of them slaves went to hug a cow or a mule good-by, cause they had tended it or worked with it all its life.

But . . . Always was called. Folks not off workin on jobs hustled into their broken-down shacks . . . gladly. Always looked round for Plum, but Plum was off somewhere, probly pullin weeds or some small job. So Always dried her hands, smoothed her apron, straightened her back, took a scared swallow, and went to the big house to the Mistress. She was newly sixteen years old with the heart and backbone of a woman, but no new wisdom to help her face this life. To get her ready for whatever might come.

She finally stood before Young Mistress, who

was writing on a sheet of one of the papers scattered on her little desk and did not look up at first.

The Mistress was not soft-hearted, but she was not truly hard-hearted. She was doing what she had to do for her own survival. She was human and she felt a few pangs of sorrow for this girl she had known since she was a baby. She spoke in a hushed voice, avoidin Always's eyes. "You have been sold to Mr. Doak Butler. He's gonna be takin you with him today. Get yourself ready. Just leave your job as it is."

Then Mistress forgot her small sorrow and wondered who else she would get to do the good job that Always did, not always playin but really workin hard.

Always's face just sorta turned to wood or stone as all kinds of thoughts scrambled through her mind. But she said a automatic "Yes'm."

Young Mistress gave Always her attention again, cause she really did need that money. "Go on, hurry now, the gentleman is waitin."

Always asked gently, "Scuse me, mam, want I go find Plum?"

The Mistress thinked on the fact that Plum and

Always was sisters. Underneath her upbringin she did feel sad again for a minute. She said, "No, we will take care of that." Then, she thought a minute, and said quickly, "You have been in this house . . . You been born here. Your pappy and your mammy was raised here . . . died here. At any rate, this has always been your home. You have been well fed and cared for. You are young and strong. You have been taught to do all kinds of work that will help you get along in the world and please your new owners. You are . . . not . . . pretty, but that is not necessary in your life and I don't think you need to be very smart to do the work you will do. Simply do what you are told to do, as well as you possibly can, as we have tried to teach you. Are you a virgin?" She knew she had no sons, but slaves were savages no matter how meek they looked. She also thought of her husband and disease.

Always nodded.

The Mistress continued. "Good! Now, I have told your new owner you are very good in the kitchen and laundry and you sew . . . some."

Always still thought of Plum. "And I takes care

of my little sister, Plum, mam. I can get her
ready."

Young Mistress stood and said firmly, "I told
you, we will take care of that."

Always thought she meant they would get ole
Miz Elliz to get Plum ready. After all, they knew
Plum was sickly, and all she had. Surely they
would not separate them. She left.

As she went down the steps to the path runnin
through the tall trees to the slave quarters, she
hated the Master and Mistress with a full heart.
But it was a useless hate, like a raindrop hatin a
tornado, just worthless and useless to itself even.
When she got to her shack she stood on the dirt
floor in a blur of tears . . . and fear. Useless.

She had shared that shack with two others, but
they were not there now. One sold last month,
one in the field somewhere. She stopped dead still,
heavin her breath, hands at her side, feelin the
thump, hearin the beat, of her heart. She looked
round the shack . . . her home. Now, now, there
was things she loved in it.

She finally went and rolled her few nothins in
a old rag. Her main piece was a head scarf she had

made out of scraps left over from sewin for Loretta and Virginia and some of the slave things at Christmas. It only took a minute to get her things.

Then, she moved in the dead silence to the square cut out in the wall for air. There she had stood many times lookin out toward where freedom might be. Where Sun might be. Where peace might be. The day was already hot with the late morning sun, when the heat thickens, grows heavy, and everything is caught in it. Through her tears and the hole-window, everything looked like it was burnt in the minute, like time was standin still. Trees, bushes, vines could be seen through that hole back of the shack. A bush with flower buds grew up and through the crooked-cut window-hole, comin between some of the loose boards of the wall.

Always's eyes filled with tears. Silent hard tears that did not roll nor move. She put out her arm and her hand sought a leaf, a little flower bud and pressed it to her nose. The smell was free. It moved gently from her nose down through her whole body—she felt hollow. Then . . . then her tears moved, flowed, and the trees and bushes, buds, seemed to wave and drown like in a dream. Everything ran together. A bird my baby threw crumbs to, from her own crumbs, flew up and landed in that budded bush. He chirped for his crumbs. There was none.

Always lifted the crushed flower bud in her hand, said, "I don't have no food to give you today, but I'll give you some love, little bird," and dropped the young petals down to the free bird. "Take good care yoself." Then she turned, picked up her rags, left her home of sixteen years. Sobs now findin their way out, tears droppin all over that shack's dirt floor, runnin through whatever there is of me, leavin pain everywhere I am, into the still, hot air, lingerin in the dust that floated in the rays of hot sunlight. The bird turned his head sideways, so to see better, and watched her go through the door for the last time, out into the world. And she didn't know a bit more bout where she was goin than that bird did! Left, not to seek a future, but to bow down to whatever future was comin to her. And I feel now as if I could KILL whoever thought of all this, such a horror mess, again and again. But I done felt this many times, again and again.

As Always walked toward her future down that time-worn path to the buggy waitin to carry her away, she wondered if Brother Sun and Peach were alive or dead. She did not know Sun had tried to buy her through Loretta, but that Loretta never told anyone because she did not want Always to go. She, Loretta, wanted to go. And Always was a kinda insurance that Sun would be where she, Loretta, could somehow reach him, and if he never sent for her, then Always had no right to get away. This . . . and still Loretta had kindness in her heart for many other things. But, I guess all these things led somehow back to herself.

I watched all these things. I knew things, and then again, I didn't know things. This bein here and not bein here all at the same time was a hard thing to be. I couldn't help nobody or nothin! It is surely a hard thing to be. And not know why . . . or even how. I only knew I couldn't help my babies. None.

CHAPTER 6

ALWAYS REACHED THAT buggy-wagon standin in front of the Big House, lookin for Plum. Plum was not there. Truth is, Plum was stealin time playin in round that ole broke-down chicken house she and Always set in sometimes to be alone together.

They told Always Plum was not goin with her and Doak, seein the look on her face, took her arm to push her up on the wagon bed. Always struggled away, cryin for Plum. Plum heard her and came runnin on her weak, little thin legs fast as them legs could carry her. An instant's look and everything was clear to even my little five-year-old Plum. She started screamin too. The yard was empty of slaves cept for those who were sposed to be out there, like the horse-handler and the buggy-man.

Young Mistress was standin in the window watchin through the curtains. Always raised such a fuss, long with my little Plum, that the mistress moved way from the window. My children cried and screamed and reached out for each other, both held back by unfeelin arms. Ahhhh, my children, my children.

Loretta continued watchin from her window, thinkin how far Always would be away when she, herself, laughed in Sun's face for leavin her behind so long. Virginia watched, then decided to run outside and help em with the black bitch.

It was when Virginia ran out the front door and all hands holdin Always turned their eyes to her, that Plum pulled away and ran around and under the wagon. Pullin herself up on a bar that fit under the seat and crossed from each wheel, Plum lay there with the stirred dust and old dirt flyin round her, into her nose and mouth as she breathed heavy and as quiet as she could. I don't know what they call it, but she lay stuck in that place til they finally brought Always down, tied her hands behind her and chained one of her feet to the sideboard . . . and drove away.

Oh Lord, I could not reach my child Plum.

As they drove along, she began to slide and somethin that damn man did drivin cause the rod to move and press into my baby child. She was too stunned and afraid to scream, thinkin too, she would be taken away from her sister, her family. She never did cry out then. She didn't feel the pain after awhile. When it gradually took over her whole little body and she couldn't hold it in anymore, her voice was weak and small and the wagon made so much noise they couldn't hear her crys and moans.

But . . . I did. I felt them too. Ohhhh, I felt them moans and her pain as she slid and the bar tore into my little child's arms and legs as she tried to hold tight to it . . . for life. Then her dear, sweet little body was held stuck as she bled to death all those long eighteen miles to where her new home would be in a grove, in the ground, in a grave. But, she did not die right away. She was unconscious, near death, when the wagon stopped and the new master got out and pulled Always, on her back, to the ground. God . . . why ain't you helpin them? Helpin me? What good is what you have let me do, if I can't do nothin for nobody? But who can know Your reasons?

It was broad daylight, round bout leven or twelve o'clock. Hot! Hot! Mosquitos squitin, flys flyin, birds flyin and screamin. Always screamin, bein pulled by the feet, she could see into the thickets, through the bushes on the damp, gravelly ground to the stream that all of a sudden looked like it was made of cracked glass. She had been hungry and very thirsty and thought maybe he was going to get some water. But . . . no, now she felt the damp dirt stickin to her, the gravel diggin into her skin as he drug her across it. She smelled the dirt, the clay, indeed, it was in her nose, her mouth, her eyes. Tied arms bled. Tied arms could not fight. She could not understand what and why he had to do this, this way. She had been goin to wait to see how it all turned out before she would hate him, but now . . . she hated him now. The pimply rough skin, the broken ragged fingernails, his rough hands and ways, he had hidden at the Big House. The handsome face with glittery, small eyes the color of the sky, now was ugly, ugly and hateful. She hated him NOW!

Then the sound came. A laugh of happy madness, possession. He was laughin! Stretchin her legs open wide and lookin and laughin as he dug his fingers into the tender flesh. She was beautiful . . . and she was his, his slave, his body to do with as he liked, at any time, in any place, and none to say nay.

He took her. Like the savage he and his kind accused her of bein. The hot sun shone through the tree leaves into her face. She never blinked her eyes. I felt twisted, grieved, memory, pain . . . worse than death. See . . . I couldn't help her. She looked through the leaves to the sky and wondered, between the pain, *why* she could not die. *When* could she die? Time trudged on slow, slow feet, til it was over.

When he was finished, spent, he moved off from

her, lookin at her with smilin eyes, proud and satisfied. How can a man be satisfied with what he takes, somethin not given to him? I don't know. He moved off from her, fixed himself up, then took handfuls of water and threw them between her legs. Jerked her up. Then, tried to kiss her! Kiss her! She struggled and he laughed. Then half-drug and carried her back to the wagon, left her in a heap.

They had both seen the puddle of blood under the wagon, and when he had her safely on the wagon, he stooped down and pulled at the bloody rag hangin there . . . what was left of my baby. He held it up to Always and said, seriously, "Was this that cute little nigga-gal, your sister?"

Always looked, the scream started and stopped in the same instant. There was no sound for this new pain added to so many others. Her heart just cried for this child she loved, silently. "Please Master, can we put her in the wagon? I'll clean it up. I'll bury her. That's my sister."

Doak held the bloody body bundle away from him, said, "Hell, you don't know if that's your sister nor not. Even live. Who knows what a slave does when they makin babies!?"

Always did cry a little sound then. Said, "Master, sir, that's my sister. I knows it. Can I have her, please?"

Doak pulled straw and whatsomever together on the wagon bed and put the body on it. "You sure betta clean this wagon up, sure nuff, cause blood is hard to come out and it looks ugly. Wonder what your old Mistress is goin to say bout this slave bein gone and dyin."

From her own bloody body and clothes, Always said, "I'll clean it up good, Master." Then he got in the wagon and finished them few miles home. Her new home.

Always bowed her head, and heaved them sobs inside her body that millions of people what was slaves to other human people have heaved down through all these centuries I feel in this huge space round me. All kinds of people. All kinds.

CHAPTER 7

ALWAYS HAD, from her first walkin and seein times, loved trees and flowers, sunshine and birds and things. Now, lookin at the yard and shabby fence of her new home, she felt nothin but a weary emptiness. The trees looked mean and broodin. The yard was like a empty, dead desert full of death. There was no comfort in the huge trees full of birds. They looked stiff, unreal and unfriendly, like the whole place had been lost and was just standin there to become her grave, not her home. She looked at the land where it stretched out, tryin to see the end of life.

Doak was proud of his nigger-slave and now he looked at his land and felt himself to be almost rich gentry. He grinned, stretched out his arm, pointin, wavin at his land. "This here is all mine! Thirty-five acres! Good soil! And we gonna fix this house up too! I got a new wife comin! Your Mistress!"

Always looked at the land through pain and hooded eyes and hate. Doak said on, "Right now it don't show up so good, just two men and," his voice hardened, "one of them a useless cripple."

He looked at Always thoughtfully. "But with a wife, and you, a sturdy slave with a lotta good years and strong suckers in you, we gonna one day stretch out to far as you can see!"

Always looked down to her sister Plum, dead. What did she care where land reached to. She hated that Plum had to be buried in this bastard's land, but it would only have been a little better back at SwallowLand where she had come from.

New thoughts was new things to my Always, but now she had some. She raised her eyes, again, to the land. A place, a secret place, she would find to bury her little sister, the end of her family. And that secret piece of land she would make hers. She'd steal it!

And she thought, "I won't work these fields. They can kill me, but I won't work these fields. I want to die anyway. I hate this man, I hate his wife, I hate his land and I will hate his children and all they children too." Then, a even newer thought struck her. "I will live. I will live to destroy them like they's destroyed me and my mama and my family." She looked at the land again. "I'm gonna destroy you too." The gust of power from the hate left her as sudden as it had come. She felt her emptiness, her bein without any power . . . and she bowed her gritty, bloody head over toward her bloody baby sister and cried all over again, inside her soul, not with her eyes.

The wagon pulled into the yard, the man, Doak called out "Poon!", and soon a older black woman came limpin down the backsteps through the yard to the wagon. She was lookin at Always, to see was this new thing come to make life harder or better.

Poon was bout thirty-five years old, lookin fifty. Nineteen children born and sold to buy most of the land the Butlers had. Scars showed for the minutes she hadn't been useful or been tryin to fight off her Masters. Lines, deep lines, from the times she had given birth to her babies, alone. Her babies?! No, just babies. No, was *her* babies. With no help. Hemorrangin, goin back to work in the kitchen, or the field, cause there was nobody else to do the work. There wasn't one soft line in her gray old face with the droopin, sad, dark round eyes filled with sad memories and questions. Where was them babies?

She did not dislike Always; she did not like her either. Just almost nothin left in her for feelins. But she was glad there was another woman here now to bear some of the burden and strain of her life.

She was a dark, ashy brown color. Head wrapped in a flour cloth rag, dress many times patched and soiled with many days wearin without a wash. She was barefoot. Body bent . . . from old pain. Her soul was bent from old pain. But . . . there was somethin. Her eyes were not broken, only sad. Or was it hate in em? Always did not know, or care. She was too full of her own hate and pain.

She slowly turned her eyes from Poon, said, "Master, I has to bury my sister, please suh."

Doak looked over his shoulder at the body and groaned, "Oh, yea. Well . . . be quick bout it. Poon will show you where. Then you get on back here to the kitchen. We need a new taste of food in this house. Poon don't try hard no more." He had a better thought. "Say, you come in the kitchen now, and bury that body later after your kitchen work is done. Then Poon will show you where she buried her dead-uns."

Who can argue with fate? Always whispered hoarsely, "Can I cover her up? From the flies? Master?"

He was down from the wagon, mind on somethin else. "Can't nothin hurt her now, get on."

She went. And the hate took stronger root in my daughter's belly and began to grow stronger in her mind. That mind that tried to plot, to scheme, but unused to havin a real goal, it didn't know how. It lay in wait. Time . . . it said . . . time.

CHAPTER 8

ALWAYS MOVED SLOWLY, painfully, down from the wagon after the chain was loosed. Poon watchin her, knowin what had done happened from the way the girl held her body.

Poon was thinkin, "She is a pretty one, oh Lord. A new wife and a new pretty nigga woman. This house gonna hold hell. Both probly weak, cain't work none. Both probly be uppity. This one won't want to work, not in the fields anyway. She ain't gonna like it here none. Ain't no pretty clothes to put on and prance in . . . and ain't gonna get ne'er ear-ring for them little pink ears, neither one."

Her heart softened at the sight of the young girl struggling to hold herself up, but her heart had too much experience to give in too soon. "I ain't gonna work for her, no Lord. I rather go on and die." Then she caught the body of my young Always, remembered the pain and the body of the young sister to be buried. Said, "C'mon in here wit me, chile. What's your name to be called?"

"Always."

"Always. That a kind of foolishness name. But mayhap you was named right . . . cause your life always gonna be just what it is now, here, where you is. And I can't help you none." She was helpin her then to walk. "Cause I got Masr Jason to watch after. He the cripple one where you can see it, and that mos take up all my time now, and we is soon again to be movin into that big shed when it finish bein fix over. Two rooms and a kitchen. I cooks for him and me only. You have the whole house to yourself to keep up. Now that the new wife is comin, the Master and his new wife is yourn."

Always took a deep breath and started up the backstairs. "When the new wife gonna be here?"

Poon helped her through the door. "A week or somethin close like that. And I's tired. Don't need nor want no young white wife-woman runnin me everywhere and doin everythin. And I'm tellin you like I'm done tol Masr Jason, when I can't do no more, when my body come down sick and cave in on my left side and I can't move, then you have to do for Masr Jason too."

Always looked up at her, then back at the fields and trees, then round the half-kept kitchen, and didn't say nothin. Just stood up straight as she could and walked on in that house. Poon went back outside to throw somethin over my poor little, dead Plum. And that was Always's home-comin.

In a short time Always healed over. She had to. It was the way of her life. In the care of the house which was really still poor, Always became a greater benefit to all everybody. Bringin in wood and kindling fetched from the woods for the fire-places and cookin stove. With her sewin, soon clothes were mended and clean, all of them. She could cook most anything and with seasonins make a poor meal a good one. She wanted a garden so she gathered manure from any livestock for fertilizer. She fed all the livestock near the house, without bein asked, and milked the few cows. She did these things to keep her mind busy, to keep from thinkin of her family gone.

She made a cross and planted little flowers round Plum's grave she had made in a little quiet grove way from round everybody else. Just hers.

The new wife was due the second week and Doak went to fetch her to her new home. Always cleaned all the bedding, killin the vermin that was there. Things wasn't rich, but they was clean and neat.

The crippled man, Jason, had a kind heart and he soon adored her. Poon, who had waited to see just what to do, began to like and help her. Jason grew to feel a little better, and sometime Poon smiled. Always made the house to seem prosperous. She looked over the land, always. But she talked to and confided in no one. She just looked over the land, always.

Doak just used her on several of the few nights

before he left to go get married and bring his wife home to his bed. When she left his bed, she always stopped to look out over the land before she cleaned herself and went to her mat to sleep.

Once, when she was through with kitchen and cleanin chores, she stood on the backsteps and looked over the land a long, long time. It was poorly tended at the time by a few hired labor. Then, she went to find a hoe and went out to the land to work it, to see and feel it. The sun was hot upon her back, the sweat began to drip from the sides of her face to her breast as she hoed in good rhythm, easily, smoothly, turnin the dark, rich earth over. She stopped now and again, bent to feel and turn the soil in her hands, feeling it was good soil. Ever once in awhile she would look thoughtfully over the land. Finally she braced the hoe on her shoulder and walked slowly back to the house, put the hoe away. Never sayin a word to anybody. Just thinkin of what the land could bear.

Sometimes, when the Indians round the area pass through from the hills for whatever their own reasons was, she give em some water or some things out the garden and talk awhile to em. You see her stoop down and scoop up some of that dirt, hold it up to em so you know that's what they talkin bout. One old handsome man specially. Papago, a kind of medicine man, became her friend. He help her a lot tellin bout the land, roots, plants and things. He just only always complain bout the fact it used to be Indian land but was all takin way but the hills. They got to be such friends, it got so when Papago's wife have a baby, Always would see to send her somethin for herself or the baby. Well, they was all poor, didn't make no difference what race you was if you needed help them days, for most people. So, her knowledge grew bout the land.

CHAPTER 9

WASN'T NO HUSTLE and bustle but a little when the wife came. A clean bed had been readied. A good meal was prepared. It was a tired, crippled group who was waitin to receive the bride. No one was goin to the door that always stayed unlocked anyway.

Masr Jason didn't want to be wheeled to the front in that ole homemade chair when they heard the wagon pull in. Poon fussed him into goin cause it was a new sister acomin. He was shamed of his body and didn't never blive, no, he knew he would never bring home a bride. He was stuck with Poon, who, thank God, cared for him well. So when she fussed with him, he allowed hisself to be wheeled to the front yard. They had already moved into their homeshed, a neat country three rooms. They just stayed in the front yard so Poon wouldn't have to pull them steps.

Always stood behind the freshly laundered curtains til the bride was steppin up to the porch. Everybody already done said "Welcome." Masr Jason was bein wheeled back to his shedhouse. The new little bride looked so nervous, innocent and even a little scared, that Always couldn't decide what kind of Mistress she was goin to be.

Sue's dress was not the best, but was a good one. Her bags were adequate, only, and there were few of them. Her hair was dark, long and wound around her head in thick braids. Her eyes were dark, and now large and round, tryin to see everything and be Mistress of it all, as ALL as Mr. Doak had described it.

Something in her face, bright, freckled, young, made Always narrow her eyes and prepare to hate her. But the hate did not come. Instead, she looked at Doak with that hate. When she looked back at the young Sue, she felt sorry for her.

She went out then to welcome her just as Doak called her name, "Ally." He didn't like the name "Always", too long, he said.

"Yes suh. Here." She came to stand on the porch.

"This your new Madame."

"Yes suh."

"Mrs. Sue."

"Yes suh. Howdy, Mrs. Sue."

Sue sounded glad to see the girl. "Howdy do, Ally."

"Name is Always, if you like, Miss Sue."

Doak spoke up as he carried the bags in. "Ain't no Miss Sue, is a Mrs., a Madame. A Mistress of Butlerville." He came up behind his wife. He looked gently at her. He loved her. She was his pride. And he was faithful to her til her sickness forced him to Always and others. He truly loved her. He was tender, gentle, and kind to his wife all her days. She never once, or more than once, thought he was unfaithful to her tho she worried a bit at first from all she had heard of gentlemen and pretty slaves. But, she was in turn wholesome, and she loved Doak as time went by. She gave herself to him with joy and lived in pleasure and peace til her end, which was not far off, as is almost always when you are happy. Listen at me. The end is almost never far off any time at all!

Now, even in the happiest house there is what is called shit. But, she was good, he was happy. He was good to her, for her, around her.

Sue became pregnant in one week really. Always was pregnant from the start. She knew it, but she didn't tell . . . yet. So they conceived little more than two weeks apart. Yet . . . he loved his wife. He didn't even think of Always.

Sue was lonely for the first month or so. Lonely for her family and past life, friends and things familiar. She really did not miss them, but she thought she did. Seems then she settled into her new state of Mistress of her own home and slaves. She tried to be busy, even to help Always in the kitchen. Her upbringin had prepared her for cookin and sewin things. But Doak didn't like his wife actin like no slave, so she finally stopped tryin, cept when he was gone sometimes. She and Always became kind of friends, tho Always spoke little.

Sue was sure she was goin to have a baby by the second month of her marriage and she was happy. Always was the first person she told.

Always had just washed Sue's long dark hair and was combing and preparin to plait and roll the thick braids around her delicate, but sturdy, head. Sue was sittin in her quiet and reserved way, lookin out the kitchen window. She turned her head a little toward Always when she spoke to her.

"This farm, the land is goin to do well someday, isn't it?" For by now she knew they were only a little above poor. "I mean, it's goin to be a good producin, rich farm someday, isn't it?"

Always looked at the top of the smooth, dark hair, the color of her own, but Always had small waves in hers and kept it tied up in her rag. She was, even already, jealous of the land tho it was rightfully Sue's land. Her thoughtfulness made Sue turn even further round to look up at Always.

"I mean, do they work it right and do things

accordin to the seasons?" Always still did not answer right away.

"Well," Sue continued, "Ain't Doak, Master Doak, seein to all that? Oh, he got so much to do! And to have only a cripple brother to help him is almost just like no help at all. Tho I do love Jason, he is so sweet and uncomplainin."

Now Always answered, as she drew the brush through the damp hair. "Yes mam. But Masr Doak need more help. Them few mens don't hardly work none when he gone."

"Well!" Indignant. "Does he know that? What can we do about it?"

Always had already thought about that. "Get Masr Jason on a horse, tie him to it and set him out to overseer things."

Sue turned full round, stoppin Always from workin her hair. "Oh, but would he do that? Could he?"

Always looked down at the truly young face, thinkin all there was in life this woman did not know. All the hard things nobody should have to know. She brushed the thoughts aside. "I blive he could, but I don't rightly know. I's just a slave, mam." Then she looked through the window at the land. "But I blive he might try . . . if it will help the land to bear better." She started brushin again.

Sue waited a moment thinkin she should save this new knowledge for her husband, but her happiness made it impossible to hold in. "Because . . . because I am going to have a beautiful baby visitor. And I want my baby to have somethin someday. So she won't have to . . . Cause she deserves it!"

Always knew she should be showin excitement and be happy with the new mother-to-be, but she couldn't gather up the gumption to act excited. She looked down at the small, frail body of Sue, then at her own strong one. "How far long is you, Mistress?"

Clappin her hands and countin on her fingers, Sue said, "Bout seven weeks, I reckon. Just bout seven weeks!"

"I's with a baby myself, Mistress," Always sighed.

Sue turned round in the chair again. Many thoughts crossin her mind at the same time; No male slave on the land, cripply Jason, where did

Always get her baby? All the tales wives of slave-
ownin husbands justa runnin through her mind.

"Who . . . where is the father of your baby,
Always?"

Always answered truthfully. "I don't know,
Mistress." She did not know where Doak was at
the particular time.

Sue turned back round, breathin relief. "Well."
She thought, "I didn't blive Always was like that,
but that is what they say bout em, and it must be
true. They have many men . . . that way, even
strangers. "How far long are you, Always?"

"Bout two months, Mistress."

Sue raised up and round one more time. "Musta
got . . . that way just fore you came . . . here."

Always knew her place. "Yes'm." And pinnin
the last pin, went to put the things away.

Sue sat a minute, lookin through the window
at the land. "Well . . . Anyway." She placed her
hand over her stomach, thinkin, "My baby gonna
inherit land and money someday. Poor Always's
baby always gonna be poor and a slave." This she
thought with no malice, even had a little pity in
her heart. But a mother's first thought is of her

own. She didn't say, "I will set you and your child free someday and give you a little land." She just felt a little pity. That's all.

Now, when all the chores was done and the workday was endin, Always and Poon had taken to sittin on stumps in front of that shedhouse of Masr Jason's. They would sit quietly or talk soft and slowly of things, just to have some company, I reckon, where they didn't have to say Masr or Mistress, could just talk.

Always spoke of the Mistress's baby that was comin. All Poon thought of was another mouth to call out for more work and was glad she was not livin in the main house nomore. She didn't dislike the new Mistress, she just didn't feel nothin and didn't like to think of somebody with more power over her, man or woman. "A baby" was all she said.

Always looked through the darkness into yonder somewhere. "I am gonna have Master a baby too." Poon just looked from yonder into the darkness. She did not smile, her own memories of her babies stayed too painful and close.

Always smoothed out her apron, said, "I sho

would want you all to help me fix that ole chicken house into a place for me . . . and my chile. Don't want to live in this house . . . with em."

With thoughts of amazement, Poon asked, "You loves him? Masr Doak?"

Always pressed her lips together in a frown. "Loves my own. Wants my own room for me and my chile, that's all. Got to live here til I die, so wants to live in my own room. Maybe soon they be havin more childrens. I'll be already done moved and that give the new Mistress time to fix things for her babies."

Poon just looked at her. "You somethin, chile."

Still lookin through the darkness, Always said, "And I wants my own garden to work."

Poon mused, "This good land. You get a good garden, good fruit from this land. It's mos pure-dee new. Ain't harly worked none. Grow yo own food to eat."

Always, still lookin into the darkness over the land, said, "I'll eat what food everybody else grows and eats. I want silver money to come out from my garden. I wants silver and gold money from what I grow."

Poon just sighed. "You somethin, chile. Don't you know what you is and where you is?"

Always got up, smoothin her apron, preparin to leave. "They can't slave my wishin none. I can try."

Another evenin, soon after that one, Always went over to sit awhile with Poon again. Always quietly said, "I blive they gonna ask for Masr Jason to sit a horse and watch the workers on the land. They ain't workin too good without overseein. Can he sit a horse? If'n he tied to it?"

Poon was alarmed and protective of Jason. "He don't need to be puttin to doin all such as that! He a sick man! That Masr Doak." She lowered her voice. "He goin too far now! Sides, them mens doin alright."

Always spoke, still softly. "No, they ain't. They lazy . . ."

Poon said, "They tired."

Always smoothed her apron, said, "We got to eat and prosper, are we always gonna be livin like this? You in a shed carin for a cripple. And if he die, you be back out in the fields again this time."

Poon was thoughtful.

Always went on talkin. "Some of them mens sleeps in the shade trees when they left alone. Them the ones eats more'n their share of the food I takes out to em. And then, somethin else more, they steals some of the harvest every day and takes it to they own shacks to cook and they already been given rations."

Poon rebuked her. "You acts like this is your fields and your food!"

Always answered, "In a way, they is. Yours too. We depends on them fields for our livin. We could have a betta livin if the land bring in more."

Poon never in her life had thought like this and it took time for her mind to grab what Always was sayin to her.

Always continued talkin. "I wants more. We all wants more. Jason wants more. Mistress is goin to have a baby child. They gonna need more room. I wants to get a start on fixin up that ole chicken house not bein used. It's big, an can be a one-room shack for me, an I still be close nough to the main house for them to call, do they need me."

Poon understood that. "The chicken house?

What you gonna fix it up with? Who gonna take time to do it? Sho can't take them slaves out the field you so busy worryin bout!"

"Fix it with all what's left over from you-all's shack. Fix it myself. Done watched em fix yourn. I can do it. Take longer, thats all."

Poon took a disbelieving breath. "I declare on God, you sho is somethin I ain't never heard of. I blive you think that light skin of yourn make you white as them is! How you gon get Masr Doak to let you make a garden and make money from it? His land!? And just what make you blive he gon let you build you yourn own room, even if it ain't in nothin but that ole chicken house? Either you a fool or you crazy! If you blive you white, you crazy!"

Always made a ugly smile. "Naw . . . I don't. Least I ain't that crazy! But, I makes me whatever I can. For my chile, for myself. I think of a way. Lots of slaves has they own shack. And they own gardens."

Poon understood that. "To eat on, not to sell and get money on."

Always spoke quietly. "Well maybe I start somethin new. But it please me if you don't talk none bout it til I find my way to it."

Poon stirred on her stump, she had been thinkin of tellin it, and laughin, to Masr Jason.

"Sides," Always continued, lookin toward Poon out the side of her eyes, "I can share it with Masr Jason and you. Masr Jason need somethin to do, build up his arms and strenth. He can help work it, it bein close to the house."

Poon opened her eyes wide in the dark. "First you got him sittin on horses and bein a overseer. Now you got him workin in YOUR garden on his land! You somethin, chile!"

Always stood up to go. "You can work with me and better your life too . . . or you can tell all I say and mess with my plan . . . but . . . every somebody with any sense wants what's better. Silver look good in your pocket as it do in Master's. Freedom talk still."

Poon cut her off. "Shush, chile! Ain't you got no sense? At all?"

Always moved close to Poon. "Don't Masr Jason read them papers Master Doak bring home?

Ain't you clost enough to him, for all you do, to get him to teach you how to read so you can read to him fore he go to sleep at night?"

Poon laughed shortly. "What I'm gonna do with readin knowledge?" She looked off cross into the darkness. "I usta, once or twict, want to learn to read. But now, I'm old. Readin ain't gonna do me no good, no more."

Always leaned closer. "You ain't dead. And slavin can kill you. You ain't sold again . . . yet . . . and readin can help you. Somethin in your head worth as much as silver in your pocket . . . sometime. Ask him!"

Poon. "It's gainst the law."

Always. "What he care bout the law? He a white man."

Poon. "You ain't gonna get me killed."

Always. "Ain't tryin to. Tryin to get you to better . . ."

Poon. "Well, leave me be. I'm doin alright. I got my own house now."

Always. "Masr Jason house."

Poon. "Mine too! And I don't have to answer all them calls no more. I don't have to tend to

115

Masr Doak's bed, just Masr Jason . . ." She stopped talkin and started in the shack.

Always spoke the last words.

"Masr Jason may die, then where you be? Get him teach you readin . . . then, you teach me. Someday, I pay you back."

Poon went on in the house and Always went on to the main house, stoppin by way round to the chicken house and seein in her mind what it could be.

The next day she began to gather stuffs to fix it, puttin by. Bout a week later, Poon, one day, held a scrap of paper up to Always, say, "That's a A, that a B, and that a C. Ain't they strangest?" Always took the scrap and studied on it, rememberin some of the things Sun had taught her. She slept with it and finally stuck it in her mouth, chewed it and swallowed it and smiled. She already knew some from what Sun had taught, but this learnin over again made it easier and quicker for her.

Mistress Sue didn't mind Always move to the fixed-up chicken house. Just took Always's hand and said, "I don't want you far away, I need you close. The time is goin fast and my baby is near to bein born . . . and I'm scared. Oh, truly, I am frightened. My mama can't come, she's down sick. My daddy wouldn't be no use, and my sister is havin her own. It's only me and you." She looked at the fullness of Always's belly that matched her own. She could never decide whether to resent it or not, but her heart was not full of malice, so she threw the thoughts away. "Your time near, too. Poon will be some help. But I want you, only you, to help me."

Always pressed Sue's hand in return. She had grown to like this woman with the kind heart. "Don't you be worry your mind, you gonna be just fine. I done asked questions bout babies comin from everybody I can walk to round here. I know aplenty."

She had walked to the closest farms askin questions bout babies. While she was there she also found out bout things planted and growin. Any different things. Bout seeds and catalogues for Masr Butler, which she knew seeds would be in. She asked bout recipes and things wanted but not found in that region. She tried to learn everything she could. She was already up to Z in the alphabet and could read small words and spell out long ones. She was learnin. My child. Doak let her walk about because she was on Mistress business.

My space, where I was, was warm and proud of my child-woman. See? I knew freedom was near, I could see it from here. I wanted her to live, and my grandbaby. Of all the grandchildren I was to have, and did have by Peach, this one of Always was already my favorite. Sun was still workin his way.

CHAPTER 10

IN THE MEANTIME. From time to time, and I didn't know much bout my kind of time early on, when I would think on one or other of my children, swift as a second I find I am where I can see the one I'm thinking bout. That's how I knew Peach was doin alright.

Thinkin hard on Sun, one time, I found myself where he was and stayed for a while.

Sun, still young, had been scrounging and makin his way north for some two years. Workin here and there for practicly nothin. Doin odd jobs all along his way from the time his little money ran out. His bein white-lookin helped him a lot and he could read way enough to understand which way he was goin and many other things.

He had reached a place near some water with beaches. Layin on the beach one day, havin swum in his clothes for a bath, he got hungry as usual. The season musta been bout over for swimmin cause not many peoples was there and the food stands was not always open. But hunger can see things when satisfied can't. Sun spied one with a man walkin round it and in and out of it, so he went over to see what he could do to get some food in him.

The man was just a-walkin and cussin and fussin, picking one thing up, settin it down only to pick up another and do the same thing. Sun was bout seventeen then. He was growin tall and hard times made him look older, even tho the young sunshine in his face told he was very young.

He greeted the white man in a mannerable way and asked him if there was some job he could do in exchange for food. The man ignored him after a mean glance. After a minute, Sun asked again.

The man found his voice, which had a foreign accent, and ranted and rowed about people always be able to ask for somethin, but never able to do anything worthwhile to get it. "Just look at this place! A mess! I can't get no cook to come and stay and work without them cheating me. Stealing me blind! Eating up my profit or giving it away to their friends. Then, leaving! They even leave sometime with the door open, so anybody can come in and help themself to anything that may be left."

Sun just stared at him and round the good-size stand. It was for sandwiches or somethin like that, and french fries. I never heard em called that, we just called em fried potatoes.

The man went on talkin with his strange accent that turned out to be French. "I'm not gonna take it anymore! I'm gonna close the damned stand and just keep the restaurant in New York I run myself. I'm sick of this American business shit!"

Sun just started movin around pickin up things

for the man. He was still listenin as he put em on the nearest convenient spot, piling dirty pots and pans in the sink.

The man just kept talkin, but began to pick up and place things with a little more thought to his actions. Said, "I tried them all: church people, no-church people, women and men, all. The church people were sometimes the worst of them all!"

Sun ran dishwater and rolled up his ragged sleeves. He sure did know how to do any kind of hard work. What he was doin now was easy to him. He asked the man, "How you make one of them san-whiches?"

The man looked at him, "Where you been, kid?"

Sun answered, "Nowhere."

The man looked at him harder. "How old are you?"

Sun answered, "Twenty."

The man laughed, "Twenty!"

Sun asked again, as he kept plowin his hands to the shoulder almost, into the soap suds, washin dishes and pots and pans. "How you make them things what you sellin?"

The man said, "Okay. You doing some work. I didn't promise you no thing . . . but you doing some work, I tell you. If there anything left to show you with, I show you. Then I clean up, lock up and go. I'm sick of this problems."

Sun said, "Show me. If I make a mistake, I'll eat it."

The man stopped and suddenly laughed. "You not smarter than me, kid. I come to America a lot younger, and smaller than you are. I come through a lot . . . a lot more than you ever know, and I make it. I am only tired now."

"Me too." Sun tried to smile. "And hungry. Thinkin I eat, I won't be so tired and I'll clean up this whole place and make them san-whiches til you make me stop. And I'll sell em and give you all your money . . . and," went on Sun, "and I'll work for you three weeks for nothin but a bed to sleep and food to eat. I don't eat much. And after that, if you like me and know you can trust me, you can pay me whatever you want to pay me. And I'll work here til I die and you'll never have to worry bout closin up this here place again."

The man, whose name was Mr. DuBois, sat

down on a box and looked at Sun. "You will work
. . . for nothing?"

"For nothing."

"Three weeks?"

"Til you know you can trust me, for a bed and
food. I'll sleep right here in the back." See, he had
no place to go at all and no food at all, so for him
that would be like a fortune or somethin. Mr.
DuBois made a wry smile and got up, picked up
a wrinkled loaf of bread layin under the counter
and stepped to the sandwich bar. "See? You take
the bread and this is called mayonnaise, I make
mine myself. Maybe I show you how sometime,
if you work out like you promise. It's the best in
America. And after three weeks, if I want you to
stay, and if I trust you, I pay you fair."

Well, Sun was hungry for everything, needed
everything, and didn't have another choice in the
whole world at that moment. His happiness made
his name show on his face. He worked good and
kept that place open and did good business cause,
my son, he was a nice person and grateful. He
smiled cause he was full and he slept without wak-

ing all through the night wonderin what or who was close to him.

That place worked and the business grew even in the small time was left in that first season. Mr. DuBois then took him into the city to work with him there. Soon, a year or two, another one was opened, the third. Soon Sun was just running them, helpin Mr. DuBois. And then there were four. All different places. And Sun was paid good cause he worked good and he learned all he could.

By that time Sun knew all Mr. DuBois's family. His pretty daughter, Colette, was just a little older than Sun, and educated. She fell in love with Sun and Mr. DuBois was glad because money should stay in a family and Sun had a future there. Course, they didn't know Sun was a negro and a slave. He never talked bout that to nobody. In time, they married. I knew then Sun had his future pretty good. Because he worked hard.

But he also went to worryin less and less bout Always comin to him. She was very light, but not white . . . enough. He stopped writing Loretta bout buyin her. Wellll, I knew Sun had his future going pretty good. He would have money. And children. Little African, French and whatever all the Master had been, but, white children, new blood. I went to thinkin on Always. Pretty soon, I went back to Always, my blood.

BACK TO ALWAYS. That same ole time was still the same kind of time when I reached Always. She was sad in her heart, and alone in her mind. She worked and thought, but always with that sad, depressed hard rock sittin on her chest, lodged in her breast, just above her baby's head. She was almost through workin on her chicken-house shack. Her mind was always runnin.

Masr Jason gave her a hand when he could. Cause he was sittin a horse now and overseein most days. It was true, it brought some life back to him. He only didn't like that it took two men and Poon to put him on, tie him, then untie him and take him off. Poon had to rub and soothe his tired muscles and chafed skin. But he did it. After all, it was his farm too.

Doak was glad about the arrangement. It gave him even more time to be off and gone on whatever he called his business. Lookin over livestock, goin to dog races, rooster fights, things like that. His farm was doin better than ever and he didn't really know why, just knew it was. He wasn't really a dumb man, just not born a farmer, but was born to know he liked land and money. Knew the land could bring him money, and slaves, but after knowin that, he really didn't feel much like workin at it, just havin it. Farm doin well, pretty wife havin his baby, that was all he knew and cared about. He was gone when Always moved into her chicken shack. He was gone, again, when the babies were born.

CHAPTER 11

FIRST OFF, MISTRESS SUE came early by a week or so. Always did all the work with her swollen, heavy belly pullin her down. Heavy, heavy. She was up thirty-nine hours with Mistress Sue til that baby boy was born.

She put on the water, folded the bed back, tied ropes down each side of the bed to be pulled on when needed. Laid out all the clean rags and towels she thought they would need. Boiled the scissors for cuttin the cord. Kept layin Mistress Sue back down and squeezin her hands when she screamed. Wiped her when the sweat just poured out of that scared young woman who kept screamin for her husband that was too far away to hear her. The birth took so long, Always had to keep going out to the well to get more water for boilin. She even changed the wet, soiled sheets a few times. Had to. Heated soup for the young woman who could not eat more than a spoon or two. The woman, Sue, cried, Always cried, holdin each other, both feared of how this new life was comin. When the time got real close, Always had to hold and lift that woman and she didn't feel small nomore. She was heavy longside that weight inside her own body.

The blood gushed along with the water, at last. Hot and heavy with its odor. It made Always retch and like to vomit on the woman cause she couldn't let go her hands. The woman had strength! Always asked, "Let me call Poon!" Mistress Sue screamed, "No, no! I don't want nobody to see me like this. I only want you!" So that was the end of that. When that baby was born, Sue was screamin and Always was cryin, tears runnin down her face. But she never stopped movin, tearin rags, wipin, pullin gently, cuttin that cord, tyin it and cleanin that baby. Mistress Sue lay back, at last, exhausted and near death, tho neither one of them knew how close.

The baby, a boy, was pink and ugly as almost all new babies are. It had dark hair and what looked like dark eyes when you could see em. A fine boy. Mistress Sue shook her head, No, when Always was handin her the baby, so Always made a sling and tied him to her own chest.

When Mistress Sue was restin, Poon was called in to help clean up round things. That's when Always's pains came and she went to her shack to lay down, rest, til the pains would leave. But the pains stayed and soon her body was heavin in her cornshuck bed . . . alone. She screamed, in spite of herself, but she had bit down, again, on her already ragged lips. Poon came. She sent Poon away, even still keepin Sue's baby with her, layed to the side of the bed, while she gave birth to her own. Said she knew all what to do for herself. Just bring hot water, she already had everything else ready.

In two hours or so, Always gave birth to her baby. As fine a baby boy as ever you want to see. He had dark hair and blue eyes like his daddy. Always looked at him and smiled. She smiled as she struggled to clean him and then clean herself. She smiled when she lay both babies to her breast and fed them. Then she fell asleep. An exhausted, deep, hard sleep, which she needed so bad.

Poon woke her up hours later. Said Mistress Sue was still sleepin. She brought broth for my grateful Always. Poon tried to pull back the home-made baby blankets, but Always pushed her away, sayin, "Leave em be. Don't wake em up. You got time nough for years to see these younguns. And let Mistress Sue be. I'll feed her boy for her, cause she too weak." Poon wouldn't argue, she left to go check again on Mistress Sue fore she went to see bout gettin Masr Jason off his horse. Mumblin, "Womens and babies, womens and babies. What's all goin on round here."

Always woke during the night and lay lookin down at the two baby boys. Holdin them, thinkin.

In the early, early dawn she got up and, takin one of the dyin embers from her little fireplace, she burnt a tiny place on her hip a little bigger than the size of a good-size pin. It hurt, but the plan was made. Then she burnt her own son on the same hip she had burnt on herself. She rubbed a little soot on it, then a little healin salve she made herself. Every day she rubbed that soot and that salve on it. When it healed, it looked just like a mole, a big mole. Hers and his looked just alike. While she was doin this, she prayed Master Doak did not return. He didn't.

Each time Mistress Sue awakened and asked for her son, Always would take the blue-eyed baby to her to hold a moment. She said Mistress Sue was too weak to hold it long or to open the blanket and fondle the baby. She always took it home with her at night, or if she stayed in the main house to be close to the mistress, the babies slept with her. In this way the wound healed each day. No one knew it was there but Always. She was considered by all to be a perfect slave to her Mistress. And, in this way, Sue grew to love the little blue-eyed baby boy. Her son.

Sue had noticed in passing that both the babies looked alike. Something inside her twinged, but her faith in what Always had never said kept her from dwelling on it. Both babies were white. That was natural to her when she thought of travelers and the Master of the plantation Always had come from. Besides, she knew her son was hers because of his blue eyes.

When Doak did finally return, ecstatic at the birth of his son and the new slave-son, he ordered Always to leave his son in his house. Not outside in some nigger shack. She could always go home to tend her own as best she could. But stay in the main house til Mistress Sue was able to care more for their son, whose name was now Master Doak Butler, the Third, tho they called him Doak Jr. Doak was glad to see his wife's son had blue eyes. So there would be no misunderstanding by Mrs. Butler. Now, the burn was healed, was only a mole anyway. Always named her son "Soon." But she took care of both of em.

Master Doak, the Third, was wrote up in the family Bible and given a doctor's certificate. Soon was wrote down in the account book as a slave with his estimated value. These two sons grew up together. Played together, slept together sometimes, ate together sometimes, said their prayers together sometimes. Was friends most times. That's the reason Soon was never sold, his friend the Young Master loved him and wanted him there. So he was the one Always was able to keep with her. Her others, my grandchildren, as they was born and got to be bout five or six years old, was sold. Was four more of em; all was Master Doak's children with Always.

When the children was sold and the money used to buy more land or somethin for the land, Always named whatever was bought by the name of her child. So there was fields named Lester, Ruby, and Lark, and a whole lotta cows named Satti. But these came later, when, under the invisible hand of Always and the cripple body of Masr Jason, the farm did better and better. Grew. The fields just abundant with growth, healthy. The livestock growing and healthy. Chickens givin eggs and meat to sell. Cows givin milk and meat to sell. Money comin in. Both Always and Masr Jason cachin some away, buryin it.

While all these things was goin on, Mistress Sue got better, but she never got really well. In about two and a half years or three she was pregnant again, but she was so thin and weak still. She truly loved her son Doak and clung to him much of the time. That's another reason he got most whatever he wanted and was able to keep Soon with him.

Sue had watched Always have two more babies. She tried to think they were Jason's, cause he was gettin stronger all the time. She knew, and she didn't know, the truth. Maybe just didn't want to know the truth. She depended a lot on Always and even still liked her cause Always was loyal in every other way she could be.

That's why, too, I think, she tried to have another baby for her husband. She was giving birth to the child, a baby girl it was, and it died as she died. Never knowing what her second child was or who her first child really was. Her death liked to kill Doak. He loved his wife and his blue-eyed son.

Everyone missed her because she had been kind. But Doak grieved and grieved and grieved, and made Always move back into the house. Altho Always gave birth to his children, it was for business reasons, not for love, so he didn't count them to be much to him. They was for work, or sale.

Master Doak was miserable and lonely. Used now to a sweet white wife, he wanted another one so he could go off and leave her all the time like he done the first one. He was drinkin quite a bit in his misery and one day, after ten months of loneliness and in the middle of a drunk, he rode back to SwallowLand to seek a wife. Loretta in fact.

Loretta and Virginia grown older, were still there. Loretta, waiting for gentry, Virginia waitin for anybody her mother would accept.

He asked for Loretta's hand and it was given him so fast, he was engaged before he fully realized he had been accepted. He was asked to stay a week, they wasn't gonna let him get away, you see? Loretta didn't love him, but he was close to gentry as she had seen in a long time on her poor farm.

They gathered food, flowers, material for a weddin dress and a preacher. In a week they had a family gatherin in the now shabby livin room and they married. Virginia cut her eyes back and forth between Loretta and Young Mistress, who wasn't so young anymore, hatred justa blazin inside her narrow heart. I blive two or three old black slaves got whipped that evenin when Virginia got full of that liquor.

Young Mistress didn't care tho. One daughter was gone . . . good! Now who? she tried to think, would take Virginia? Perhaps they could get a little money from Loretta now, buy a few clothes and take a trip to meet some eligible gentry for Virginia. If she could just get Virginia to act like a lady long enough.

As for Loretta, she did not love Doak or ever think she would. She just looked down her nose, closed her eyes, and became a wife. She had given Sun up, now she hated him and through him, Always. She made Doak buy her another house slave to be her personal maid, like he had got for his first wife. They could afford that and a better carriage now because Always's plans for the farm were workin.

Loretta came in her new home, head held high, eyes searching to see everything. She saw many things she wanted changed, bettered. There was much papering of walls and painting of ceilings, even a room added and a regular room for bathing. She bought clothes for the first time in years. Lovely laces and fine cloths as they could afford. Doak was happy with his new bride til he began to count all the money going out. He fought her over a new dining room. She won that battle, not knowing how many others she was losing with that one win. He preferred his money to her from that time on.

Loretta's settling in moved everybody over more than a notch or two than they were comfortable with. She was not so liked. Not even by Jason, who tried to like everybody. She demanded everything, manners, meals with every proper settin and service. She wanted to be treated as a proper wealthy mistress and, of course, she was. She pressed Always into waitin on and serving her own maid, doing the washing and such as maids should do on their own for their selves.

Now, things had never been heaven for Always, but they had been a little better because of the kind

Sue. Sadness moved back into her everyday life and even fear. For the past was moving back into her future, and the past had not been kind. But life and time just kept movin on, like it always does. Like it always does.

CHAPTER 12

ALWAYS LIVED, when she could, for her garden. She had done all the shoppin for Mistress Sue while she was sick and Always had stolen the money, when she could, for all kinds of seeds and different small tools for that garden. It had all kinds of different vegetables and things from the catalogue. She didn't feel like she was stealin cause she worked and they didn't pay her.

Now, she sold things from her garden. All the white ladies and their cooks within twenty-five miles or so around, knew to come to her for things in season, and some, out of it. She had many different things sides potatoes, tomatoes, cabbage, and corn. There is many a vegetable and fruit! All different kinds of squash, radishes, different color bell peppers, somethin called broccoli, cauliflower, lettuces of all kinds. My child knew her land! From that small square they had given her next that chicken shack, she added a row or two each time she plowed it til it spread right under their noses. They ate some from it, but not much as they thought they did, cause Always wanted that silver to put down in that little hole in her dirt floor and walls . . . for some future, whatever it was gonna be. Silver could always be used.

Loretta, of course, checkin everything as is the duty of a Mistress, questioned the space and use of the garden and its produce. She noticed the women who came to purchase from it and demanded an accountin of the money cause it rightfully belonged to the Master. She questioned Always, but Jason provided the answer. Said Always was workin for him, and after that she kinda was, cause she had to give him some of her money.

And, too, Loretta felt like she was somehow made a fool of and her heart grew harder toward Always.

Her heart grew harder toward Soon also. To her, he looked like Sun. Ain't people strange? It wasn't nothin that boy had done to her, just she was mad at Always cause she felt used and let down by Sun, so she wanted to hurt his full sister. She was workin on Master Doak to get him to sell Soon cause Soon was a healthy, strong youngun, would bring a good piece of money.

Young Doak wouldn't hear no kinda talk like that. He pulled his own kinda tantrum round there, screamin and hollerin up so much racket, cryin and wrappin hisself round his daddy's legs, til Master Doak made it clear that Soon was there to stay and blonged to young Master Doak. That was that!

Now Loretta was not as innocent as Mistress Sue had been. Not gullible. She knew whose sons both them boys were. But she didn't know much as she thought she did cause she was really good to that boy Doak who she thought was Sue's son. Other than the tryin to sell Soon, she gave young

Doak all he wanted and more cause she was tryin to make gentry out of him, school and clothes and all like that. But Doak was a man's boy and he wriggled out of all he could.

Through the years Loretta tried to make a break between the boys. Taking every chance to show Doak Jr. he was the boss, the Master, and Soon was the slave. She gave Soon all kinds of chores to do to keep him too busy to have time to play. But Doak Jr. took to helpin Soon with his chores, so they could get back to playin. Loretta told him he "was doin nigger work cause that was Soon's work and he was the nigger!" She tried to keep Doak Jr. busy doin somethin else in the white folks line, but it got harder and harder tryin to keep up with them boys, gettin her fine skirts dirty seekin em out. She finally gave it up, mostly cause she knew the years would bring a change when Doak Jr. understood more. She had made up her mind to that. He would be goin away to school someday. Gentry, you know. And Soon would not be goin with him there!

Loretta also knew Master Doak indulged Soon, and tho she lorded it over most everybody, she didn't lord it over Master Doak. He was just gone so much, from what he called a frigid wife, she was able to do just most what all she wanted to in the house and somewhat on the farm cept for what Jason demanded be his to do. The years passed and didn't bring no change from that.

But, finally, she brought a change in Doak Jr. He grew prideful of the fine clothes his stepmother bought for him, and his nice room, his own horse, things like that. I guess he began to have to look down at somebody cause they wasn't at the very top themselves. In time, he made new friends among his "own" color, and had less and less time to spend with Soon. Sides they was gettin older and play was pass anyhow. But Doak Jr. was kind enough to let Soon take care his things for him.

Loretta finally had a small ballroom added to the house, sides a extra bedroom for herself. The ballroom was to bring her up a notch and was for her genteel friends entertainin. You had to move tables and chairs to make a decent floor for dancin, but she called it a ballroom right on.

She finally got her way in spoiling Doak Jr. I

hated to see him go that way cause he was my blood, white as he was. I wanted to love my grandson, but the circumstance kept gettin in the way. I did love Soon cause he was there with my daughter, called her mother and was a good son, had a good heart and a level head, worked hard, studied his lessons hard his mama taught him. She started not to teach him cause he was really white and she was gonna take some small revenge on him for what "they" had done to her. I watched her with grief in my heart for the shape of her heart. But she decided in her mind that he was goin to be a nigger slave all his life anyway, so he better have somethin to help hisself with. She taught him all she knew. I could see she loved him anyway. Just sometimes, the situations people build up round you confuse you and make your thinkin go all crooked and wrong. Human look like it just have to be human!

Soon was thrifty. He helped his mother on her plot of land and she paid him a few coins as she made them. He spent the money on candies at the store when they went. Then he took to savin them in his own little hole in the wall. He was quiet and thoughtful as he grew older. Often sad. He loved Always, naturally. He thought she was his mother. The only other white person he loved sides Doak Jr. was Jason, who was kind to him. He liked Poon who loved to feed him and sew his clothes. His mother didn't have time.

He was jealous, at last, of Doak Jr. and the way Always did hug and pet him and save little treats for him. Of course she shared the treats, but Doak Jr. always seemed to get the best or the biggest.

Always, herself, didn't really always know who she loved the best. She surely loved Soon. She slept with him, talked all the time with him, cared for him through his sicknesses, but so she did with Doak Jr. when Loretta let her and you can believe Loretta let her if it was somethin messy. But still, she knew who her son was, where her blood was, and that always set her actions. She was careful, but she was a mother and sometime she forgot to be the right mother for the right son.

So, time still takin care of everything, the boys grew older and apart. There's just some things a slave can't do. Doak Jr. took to belittlin Soon and playin off him round his white friends. Small sparks of hatred flamed in Soon. Musta been natural cause he sure didn't plan for em. He still loved Doak Jr. at the same time.

Doak Jr. still didn't want Soon sold tho. He knew this was in truth his brother. He liked him. But at the same time he didn't like him because he was his brother. Where once they realized moments and hours apart, as they grew older it came to be days, then weeks apart, then months. Finally they got to be bout sixteen years old. The war was pressin in. Was all the talk. That set them more apart even tho it wasn't none of Soon's fault that the war was comin, that the slaves might be freed. Howsomever, all slaves everywhere was bein looked at different, harder. Where once they was thought to be dumb and happy, white eyes began to watch for some thought, some way to know what really was goin on in a nigger's head.

Sometimes Always was hung between givin up, givin in, or goin on. What good was all that silver gonna do her in the end, she thought. Hope was hard to hold on to between weepin and grievin for lost, sold babies . . . and loneliness. Cause she was lonely, lonely sometimes for a man of her own. To help her think and live, plan plans, seek a way, any way. But there was none she could choose.

She had even looked at the Indian men as they continued to pass through over the land. They knew her now, well. They helped her in little things in her garden and sometimes brought her strange new herbs and roots to plant. They looked her over too, cause they could help her steal away. But her heart made no choice. She would not leave the land she felt was hers.

She always watched Doak Jr. with hard, hooded eyes. She watched him and she thought hard on him and tried to find a plan in him. She knew one was there because she had started one in the beginnin when he was born. But so much time had passed and she couldn't always remember it or when she could use it, if she could use it. But it was there. Somewhere.

The people filled the air and newspapers all the time now with the rumors of war between the North and South. But the South felt strong and safe within its men, so noone really worried. They scoffed and drank their toddies, loved their land, whipped their niggers, fornicated over their slave women. Laughed.

Poon could read and spell out words fairly well now, but not as good as Always. And she didn't always understand what she read. So she claimed Always used the papers for covering the walls of the chicken shack and took them over there when Jason was finished with em.

Now Jason was not dumb, but sometimes he felt more kin to Poon than Doak, so he did not make the trouble he could have. What harm could slaves do really? He didn't have a mean heart full of hate. Bitter, yes. But bitter turned inside cause of his legs, you see?

Always was bout thirty-two years old now. Poon was much older but looked better than she did sixteen years ago when Always first came. Hope was pullin Poon along. She knew more, did a little thinkin. Freedom might be close. She began to think on her lost sold babies. Mayhap she could find em! Or maybe even that man she had really liked, maybe even loved, who had made a few of them babies fore he was sold away from his home

up the road. She began to dream . . . a little . . .
again. Her dream tools was rusty, unused for years
and years, but found to be still workin after awhile.

Then . . . the war did come.

All the proud soldier-men rose at the same time
to go fight for their part of their beloved country
and women.

Master Doak, tho too old, went. Glad to go!
Didn't blive he would DIE, but turned out he DID
soon after he joined the Army. Only Jason could
not go. Only sit tied on his horse, watchin over
niggers and land, staring at the path his brother
cut as he rode triumphantly away, waving his
sword back at them. Though Always begged so
hard for Doak Jr. not to go that Loretta began to
believe Always did love them, he went.

When Always begged just a little less when Soon
wanted to go with Doak Jr., Loretta wrinkled her
brow and began to think more when she looked
at her stepson. Then Always changed her mind
and actually sent him with her blessings to be with
Doak, to watch him, to protect him, to even die
for him, she said. They left. Doak Jr. smiling and
eager, Soon thoughtful and serious.

Even under Jason, the slaves on the land grew lazy. Some ran off to fight. Fightin what? They didn't have nothin they dreamed of cept freedom. They fought well and strong. Jason, Always, and Loretta had it hard runnin the farm. Not makin it pay so much, cause you had to *give* so much to the army. But just stayin somewhere round the top of things and themselves eatin. People, white and black, stole from them now. Livestock and vegetables. All is fair, you know, in love and war.

Always kept her garden separate long as she could. She took to sellin anything she could to add to her horde of silver. She eyed Jason and Poon to see where they hid their cache. But Poon watched her and watched out for Jason.

They all watched Loretta, who was still playin high-and-mighty. Always knew where Loretta kept the silver and gold. She never touched it, but she helped to keep it safe. She kept everybody else away from it.

Time passed. Don't it always? So many things began to happen, I have to look back to tell of it and looking back is coming harder for me now. So bear with me.

A colored knife-sharpener man commence to coming through the country with his wagon. He was a brown-skinned, young-middle-age man. He struck his eye on Always, who kinda struck an eye back, cause he was one of the few freed men she had known. Added to that, he had his own business, such as it was, his own wagon. They looked and talked and laughed some, til finally all the knives and scissors at the Butler plantation was sharp as they would ever get again in life.

He really liked Always. She was still a fine-looking woman. Her industry kept her slim, her breast was full from the children she had birthed. She wore a long calico dress, or her everyday dress of sackcloth, long, so he never saw her legs cept in a quick look as she bent or raised her skirts to step up somewhere. He liked her quick tongue, her strong and flip ways. He would have liked her to smile and laugh more, but he felt he could might change that . . . if he was ever able to get closer to her. He thought of marriage, but he wasn't savin his money to buy a wife, he was savin it to buy a house, then he could carry on his trade from one place. So . . . they just looked, deep and hard, and kept talkin bout other things. And laughin. They both thought of it often tho.

Always had never liked nor loved no man before and money was really uppermost in her mind more than anything. Savin it and still not knowing just what for. But, knowing if the white folks wanted it, it must be the best thing to have. Didn't want to buy herself away because she felt this was her land she worked on. Things was not too bad now. Wasn't hardly no whippin goin on. The only thing was she cried some nights for her children what was sold and gone. She could handle Loretta or stay out her way. So, even with the war goin on, things was at the time almost alright on her plantation.

Then, one day, another man came through. Colored, but light and looked sorta like my own Sun. That's who Always thought it was at first. She ran toward the tired, barefoot man, joy in her heart. She thought this was some of her blood, her family! Til she was close enough to see . . . he was too young, it was not Sun. Turned out his name was Sephus and he was hungry. Always was used to givin what she could to the slaves that were more and more often comin by the plantation or trudging by night down the road that faced it. Running away from somebody or to something. So naturally she fed him. She liked to look at him, he looked like somebody she knew. Well, he was somebody she knew! He was lookin for his mother he had been sold from and was following this road. Do I need to tell you what she felt? They both felt? That huge joy? Only his name had been changed. But they had to be quiet about it cause the war was not over yet, didn't know who would win and send him back to his owner. So they loved in silence and touching. Always's heart overflowed so til it hurt. He did not know where her other children was tho. It's always something to remind you that everything ain't never gonna be alright!

She had just brought him some food that first day, when Loretta rushed out, slowly tho, like a lady, to see this man. She had seen him from her window and thought it was Sun, too. She had planned to hate and be angry with Sun, but her face was shining and happy to think this was him. It dropped, like a lady, and showed her disappointment when it turned out to be it wasn't him. But she stayed and watched and asked questions.

"Where your master, boy?"

Sephus had done stopped eatin and was dartin his eyes round lookin for a place to run and to see was anybody else coming. He was so hungry he was desolated, and he did not want to lose his mama again after only havin her a few minutes. He hesitated and spoke. "He dead, mam."

Loretta walked in front of him. "Who was he? Where you goin to . . . Or coming from?"

He choked on a bite. "We was agoin up to town there"—he pointed a chicken foot. "But he dropped dead . . . I'm goin on now, back home . . . to 'vise his family."

She looked directly down at him. "No, you ain't, boy! You just lyin through that food of mine you eatin!" Always thought to herself, "That's my food he's eatin and I fixed it too!"

Sephus dropped the chicken foot, stood, lookin mighty afeared. He looked at Always, who slightly shook her head, tellin him not to be too afraid.

Loretta continued talkin, "Well, anyway, if he

dead, he don't need you no more." Sephus gulped, but stood still, waiting in the little silence while Loretta stared at him. Both slaves watched her to see what she was thinkin afore they would know what to do. She finally said, "You ain't goin home a'tall! So I might as well keep you. I need a driver for my new carriage I have had for two years now, that's fallin apart in that barn yonder. Have to drive it myself sometime, and no lady should drive herself. So . . . I need a driver. Can you drive a carriage, boy?"

Well, the boy could, but he had just done run off from bein a slave at one place and wasn't lookin for no job in the South, nor of bein a slave at no other place. His mind did a few quick turns, as it shoulda, and he could see himself driving north stead of walkin there. He looked in the white woman's eyes to see what could he see there. She didn't show too much, but he saw somethin. Then he looked at his newfound mama.

"Yes'm, I can drive a carriage. That's my regular job."

"Then you can care for horses?"

"Yes'm."

"Open your mouth and say 'Yes mam,' boy!"

"Yes'm. Yes mam."

"You can eat and sleep here awhile, with no more questions bout your dead master. Dead master, indeed. If you drive good, we will see what you can earn for a little livin money."

Those last few words had Always lookin at Loretta like she had never seen her before in life. Now she took to wonderin bout why Loretta was doing this stead of callin for somebody to come take this boy, her son, back to his rightful master. And to hear her offerin him 'a little living money' was beyond anything she had even known a white person to do. She wondered was Loretta stallin for time, but she knew Loretta didn't have to stall, she could either do what she was gonna or not. That's bout where she was when Loretta turned to her. "Show him where he can bathe and get him some of Doak Jr.'s clothes. Can't have no raggedy driver. Then send him up to me."

"Yes'm, Miz Loretta," came the thoughtful, wondering reply. "Yes mam."

Sephus looked at Always to see what he should do; when Always nodded her head slowly, he fell upon his food again and didn't look up til Always was handin him some clothes and pointin the way out to the well where he could fetch water to bathe in, and then her cabin to take it in, tellin him that is where he would be stayin . . . with her. She wanted to hold him, caress him, talk to him. She was goin over in her mind when he was born, how he looked, the type of child he was. That filled her mind all the long day, and everytime she passed him for some thought-up reason, she touched him. Her son. Her son.

Sephus didn't get to stay more than one night with his mother. He became part of the main house where Loretta lived. He forgot his plan to travel on north. Tho he was fearful when he carried Miz Loretta out and around, he knew, now, she would protect him. He stayed in the barns caring for the horses or in the main house finding something to do, which wasn't hard. That lasted bout three months. Then the patrollers was gettin so thick on the roads cause so many slaves was runnin, he said he was sick and couldn't drive no more. One day, soon after that, Loretta woke up and he was gone. Gone on north. Cleaner and fatter. He couldn't pass for white, but Always had writ him a good letter that would get him through.

Both women took his leavin hard, but Always took it better because she knew he was runnin to freedom. Loretta couldn't understand because she had been good to him. Really good. Strange tho it seem, she didn't hate *him* so much, she just hated Sun more! She cried but she wouldn't let nobody see her do it. Always cried too, but she did look at the chance to hear from him, see him again, if she had to make that knife-sharpin man drive her near cross this world to do it! They was huggin a little bit now and then, on the sly, of course. Just a little huggin tho.

Sephus was gone bout a month when, one day, Miz Loretta sent for Always, needing something to ease her "flow." That her monthly cramps was very worse. Asked her for some roots or medicine that would make her flow more easy. Always gathered and fixed what she could think of, but none of it seemed to satisfy Loretta, who was becoming more irritable every day, so that Always wondered just how long them cramps was gonna last. Each day, goin on a week then, Loretta asked for it to be made stronger and stronger.

Soon after that askin day, Always was stirring and fixin a very strong potent medicine and her mind clicked into a place, thinkin. Loretta had never had troubles with her monthly time before. Not like this noway! It came to Always that Loretta was pregnant. Master Doak was gone. And dead too. "Who? Who?" Then Sephus came to mind. "Great Lord!" If that was true, then Loretta was going to have her grandchild! And she was trying to get rid of it! It sure did come to me that Loretta was carryin my great grandchile. Loretta! Then some more came to me, chile. Loretta was going to be the mother of her own nephew! Oh, I was tryin to follow my blood, know my kin, and it was turnin round on itself in some places, runnin into places it never shoulda gone to. Never! And there was Always . . . bein asked to fix medicine that would kill her own grandchile! Honey, life can get to be more than you can know.

I was tryin to watch my blood, my family, but it was gettin so confusin and mixed up! My father was Loretta's and Always's grandfather. They had the same father. Always's children was Loretta's husband's, so Sephus was Loretta's stepchild and nephew and the father of her child, which was mine and Always's grandchild and Loretta's step-grandchild and child and, oh, it can go on and on. But, anyway, if we all done come from Adam and Eve, we done always been relatives anyway. Lord, Lord.

Anyway, as Always allowed, hadn't been nobody round ceptin Sephus. All the nice-lookin white men was gone to fight the war, and the other older white men stopped to chat or came by to buy somethin or do business in some way was never lowed beyond the very front porch. Or if they was old friends, the very front parlor, with Loretta's personal slavewoman almost always present.

However, Always took the latest batch, a pint of medicine to Loretta who was in bed, languishin away. A bit unkempt for a woman who was so particular, burdened, distraughted, worried. She took the water glass from side the bed, poured a small bit into it, said, "Mam, I know this here medicine gonna work. This be bout the strongest medicine I knows how to make to make the misery go way."

Loretta reached for that glass like her arm was lightnin and swallowed the stuff right down that really did not taste no way good at all. Always watched her a minute as she smoothed the cover and things and began to tidy and puff up the pillows beneath Loretta, who she was watchin very carefully, on the sly of course.

Always picked up the bottle just as Loretta reached for it. Said, "Mam, I know this gonna work cause it's strong, strong! Ladies with child is not sposed to take none of this stuff! Course, you ain't with child cause everybody know a lady in that condition, her elbows turn dark, dark, til she have that baby." Loretta forgot herself, looked desperate at both elbows with wild eyes. Said, when she come to herself, "I have no reason to think of that, Master Doak bein dead and all. That is impossible. Leave me now. I want . . . I want to rest." Always left, but she took the bottle with her. Loretta was figitin round and didn't notice. Always went to her shack and poured out the strong medicine and made up a batch that wouldn't kill a fly. When Loretta sent for that strong medicine, which was mighty soon, she sent that new stuff.

Always watched for the next month or two as Loretta became more haggard, stayed in her room and regular sent for more medicine to take. She began wearing longer, fuller skirts. Loretta was gonna have that baby! Always, Lord help her, smiled sometime as she looked off into space. Always didn't worry bout the control this baby of Loretta's would have over the plantation, because all would know it wasn't Master Doak's, so the baby just might have nothin but a mama, if Loretta didn't kill it when it was born. Cause it was sure steady comin! Probly gonna be strong with all that nourishin medicine Always had started sendin in to Miz Loretta.

Passin, with the time, was the way of life as it was usta bein in this south. Things was more scarce, but Always had a good cache of things and Jason was no fool and had been lookin ahead to these times hisself. They was holdin on for everybody, that cripple and that slave.

The roads was full now of slaves goin one way, and crippled and maimed soldiers, and some runaway soldiers too, goin another way, mostly in the nights. Always kept little packages, the little she could give away freely, ready for the slaves when they came knockin on the windows of her shack. Word gets round and they had done heard bout her. God is good. She helped and she asked questions in return. She learned one side was winnin on one day, and the next day the other side was winnin. Facts, the slaves didn't really know all the time, but they was sure the South was losin cause of the things happinin on their old homes.

Always tried to describe her children to the runaways, but they didn't know bout them either, tho some of them sounded like they might. Then, how could they tell her which way to where the grown children might be now, when they, themselves, had criss-crossed by night the huge land? But she kept helpin and nobody bothered her, cause Loretta mighta been the only one to do it and she was so caught up in her own troubles, she didn't pay much tention to Always cept to curse her for not givin her medicine that would work!

When the day came for the baby to come and Loretta couldn't hold back no more, she sent for Always, then sent her slavewoman away. She looked haggard and resigned, like she had just given up. A little, worn thing layin and pullin the sheets one minute, her hair the next minute.

Always stood at the foot of the bed, lookin down at Loretta. "Miz Loretta, mam, I blive you fixin to have a visitor."

Loretta looked up with knowing malice. "And my elbows never did get any darker." Her face worked with the pain that struck her.

Always started to get busy. "Well, I reckon we just get ready for it."

Loretta gasped from the pain. "Hold on." She grabbed Always's hand that was foldin back the covers. "We must talk first. I have to talk to you."

"Yes mam." Always was smiling inside, but her face was serious. "You want me to send your helpmaid back?"

"No, no." Loretta drew her lacy sleeve cross her damp brow. "No, I want only you here! I want . . . I want you to do something for me."

The pain threw her head back. Always waited. "I'm . . . I'm havin a baby." She looked through the pain. "But you already knew that."

"Yes mam."

"I cannot . . . I must not . . . keep this baby."

"Oh, Miz Loretta, you be so lucky, so blessed . . . able . . . to keep your baby. I wish I coulda kept mine. I wish I coulda kept my mama . . . her mama too."

Loretta opened her eyes wide to Always. She was tryin not to scream out hatred names to Always . . . cause she needed her just then. But she did say, "You are an evil woman, Always."

"No mam, not evil. Just a slave. Witout a brain, nor a soul."

They waited in silence a minute. The past filling both their minds. But, here now, was the present, and something had changed. Then the pain hit Loretta again.

"Mam, what does you want me to do, Miz Loretta, you needs help."

Loretta fell back against the pillows. "I must not keep this baby. I don't know . . . what it will be . . . what it will look like."

"Look like you and the daddy, Miz Loretta. Like you and the daddy."

Loretta looked at Always, this time with hate mixed with pleadin, if you can magine that. "I helped your brother to be free."

"You helped our brother to be free, or dead, mam, but you didn't help him for me. And you never helped me, no way. Mam."

Loretta raised herself. "But he is free! I heard from him, a long time . . . ago."

Now, Loretta sure said the right thing. This filled Always's heart with joy, to know her brother was alive. Now, all was left was to know where. She would take her money and go to him. Even . . . even leave the land that blonged to her. Then her heart filled with pain. He had never come back for her. Or sent anyone to her with a message, a nothin. No . . . she couldn't go. But . . . "Where is he then, Miz Loretta?"

Another pain had torn through Loretta's body and she burst into a sweat at its leavin. "Always . . . I want my child. Now. It's my only child I will ever have. But I can't keep it." She bit her

lip, started cryin. "I . . . want you . . . to keep it
. . . for me. Raise it, my baby."

Always turned her head sidewise and looked
down at Loretta. "You want ME to help you?"

"Yes, yes! I neeed help. But I need . . . I want
you, to keep my baby. Let it . . . be yours."

"But what I'm gonna tell it? What it gonna call
me?"

"Mother . . . mama . . . mammy. Anything. I
want you to raise it, as your child."

"Well . . . you best let me help you get ready
now. I will think on it." Always knew she would
keep her son's child.

Loretta drew her pain-filled body up. "You will
do as I tell you. You are MY slave. You do as I
tell you to."

Always had moved to the room door to go get
things, to prepare things. "I don't have to do
nothin but die, Miz Loretta." She smiled. "I hear
tell the war is bout over. Colored folks say the
North is winnin. White folks say the South is winnin. I don't know right what to blive, but I do
know things is changin. They right in front of my

eyes. Folks is changin. White folks runnin. Grabbin their things and slaves and runnin. Don't
sound like no winnin things to me. So . . . I don't
have to do nothin no more but die." She left the
room.

Loretta sat up and screamed, "Always!"

Always stood outside the door and looked up
to the same God I was askin mercy for her from
. . . and thanked Him. She thanked Him. God
must get mighty tired of us.

Well, the baby was a girl. A tiny, tired, wrinkled, little girl. Tiny cause of all those corsets her
mama had worn to keep from showin her. Tiny
cause her mama tried to starve her. Yellow from
her daddy, Sephus. She fell into Always's arms
like she was glad to get there. Always named her
Apple, from the Bible, she thought. The apple that
Eve had bitten from. Loretta said she didn't want
that name. Always said she had to name the child
somethin she wanted cause it was hers. Little Apple moved on out to the chicken house that was
Always's home, and became Always's daughter-
child and Always knew she now had a baby wasn't
nobody gonna sell from her. Over time, Apple

grew plump and pretty, full of easy laughter. Everybody seem to love her. Even Poon didn't worry too much bout how and where she came from. She was a smart, quick child. Taught to work, early, she was weedin the garden and other small chores with Always. Sometimes Loretta had her in the main house, lovin her from a distance, I reckon, wantin her close. The two women didn't never fall out bout the child, cause Always knew what it was like to lose your child, and she was easier with Loretta. Course now, she practicly ran what was left of that plantation, with Jason in the lead, of course.

So the time passed. Many things happened. But who, not I, can tell them all? It was a long time, a hard time, a confusing time, and it was a lotta kind of time, but seldom a good time, except for hearing bout the freedom comin closer, for slaves.

One warm day, Loretta sittin on the porch of the main house, Always settin on the steps, peeling peaches and potatoes brought out from the cache. Apple playin round the steps. Everyone, includin Mistress worked now, so many slaves had run. Such a hollerin came from the road, which suddenly seemed full of strangers and stragglers, slaves, white men, young and old, poor and usta be wealthy, all moving in sort of frenzied actions. A white man on a horse galloped up to the porch and tole Miz Loretta the war was over! Was won! By the North! Said, "Watch everything you got! They'll steal it all now, for sure! Keep your gun by you! These nigras is aiming to have a white woman! But war won or not, we'll still kill em ifn they don't do right! We still white, and they still nigras!"

Loretta just looked at Always and turned red. The man had galloped off before she could even answer. When the man had rode off, Loretta's hands was still on the pot of peaches. Her eyes were fastened hard on Always. Her face held a regretful, serious look, and somethin else, like hate that Always had got freedom, and a fear of what Always would do . . . and when.

Always rose slowly. Trying to feel the feelin of freedom. Her mind screamed "I'm FREE! I'm free! I'm free!" She looked at little Apple. "We is all free!" She put the potatoes aside and started down the steps, slowly, thoughts whirling so fast in her head. She wanted to go tell everybody! Just everybody in the world. Then, she sat down again, slowly, hands stilled, lookin into the air behind the rider. There was no smile, no more free laughter from her. On the inside tho, was the explosion. Comin slow and huge, the size of the world that was bein blown apart, it felt like. Realization crept slowly, and silently into every piece of her body that had been a slave for all its life. She thought of her money, and the money she would take from the pot blongin to the Butlers, her rapist, her children's father. Not all of it, just some of what she thought she had comin, had earned. She thought of her son, Doak Jr. He had always been free, but now he really was free, of all but her. She looked at Apple, she looked at the road that went everywhere in the free world, then she turned slowly and looked at Loretta.

Loretta spoke first, "Well, them's the words you been waiting for all your life, tho we been good to you, all of us, from the day you was born."

Always answered, "Them's the words."

Loretta spit the words, "I reckon you be flyin off now, to find your brother, Sun, or your sister, Peach."

Always answered softly, "Maybe they come find me. Ain't goin off nowhere notime soon." Her eyes looked in the direction of the colored church shack.

Loretta narrowed her eyes, "You mean . . . you gonna stay here . . . to work? There ain't gonna be no pay. You know I could tell Soon where you gonna be if you go. I'll . . . I'll keep Apple so you don't have to worry none bout her."

Always thought, "So Loretta did, had known, bout the war bein lost and had thought all this out." She was fairly jumpin for joy inside her soul, but her body did not move, she still held the pot in her lap. She looked down at it, as if it were some-thin with feelins, gently moved it from her lap to the step. She said out loud, softly, because this freedom thing was movin out like water, through her mind and body, "You don have to worry none bout me, Miz Loretta, I'll find out what to do."

Loretta watched her move the pot from her lap,

her eyes glinted lightly, "Well, if you gon stay on here, you will work, and I can't pay you."

Always slowly stood up, again, shook her skirt. "You ain't been payin me."

"Things'r different now. You won't blong to us . . . for us to take care you no more."

Loretta finally got through Always's full, free mind. She looked at Loretta. "You never did take care a me. All us slaves took care you'll. And we never did blong to you, you just kep us, by whippin and killins."

Loretta spoke right back. "I knew no matter what we did for you, you would hate me."

Always waved her hand. "Miz Loretta, I don't think nough of you to hate you. I's too tired."

Loretta pushed on. "And Apple stays with me til she grown and decide for herself."

Always sighed. "We already decided for Apple. She mine. Don't everbody know it? And all my babies, but one, went to buy most all this land. That bout make this land mine, and Apple mine. She my real grandchile . . . so she mine, Miz Loretta."

Loretta gasped. "My daughter! A grandchile of yours?!"

Always looked up and smiled shortly. "Yes'm. And your niece too. Wouldn't your daddy be proud? Won't Doak Jr. be proud? When I tell em . . ."

Loretta spoke with hate. "You a conivin, low bred, lyin bitch."

Always looked away. "I sho didn't carry you into your bed with Sephus. I didn't carry your daddy to bed with my mama. I didn't make these things . . . you'll did."

Loretta spoke softly now. "You waited for somethin like this."

Always spoke softly too. "That's all you'll let slaves do. Work, wait and maybe hope." She started down the steps slowly, old and tired for all her young years.

Again sharply, Loretta spoke. "Where you going, Missy? Ifn you gonna stay, you best finish preparin that food! Let's get them potatoes peeled fore you go off. We got to have dinner even so!"

Always stopped on the last step. "I don't have to peel those potatoes . . . no more."

Loretta twisted her lips. "You got to peel them, do you want to eat!"

Always smiled a hard smile, "I ain't got to do nothin, Loretta, but die."

Loretta stood, peaches goin everywhere, quietly she said, "You still call me Miz Loretta, I don't care what has come. You sit down there and finish peeling those potatoes, then you will cook them, then you will clean up after we eat."

Always jumped down the last step. "No mam, I'm through today. I through this week. Through til I'm rested. I'm goin over to the colored church you never lowed me to go to. I'm goin to see is we really free. Then I'm goin to tell the others bout this freedom." She looked at the road fillin with people, slaves and all. She listened to the air, which was a lite with the buzzin sound of freedom spoken, over and over.

Loretta answered, "Then you will not eat. Come here, Apple."

Always answered, "I will eat, Loretta." She moved back up the step, held out her hand to Loretta. "You see this here hand? This hand helped the ground to grow the food that you goin to eat.

With these hands, I have fed you. Yes, I will eat. And Apple will come with me, cause she is colored and she need to know if she free too!"

Loretta bristled like them ladies did in the South, and tried again. "Then you will get off my land . . . and stay off my land. This is no longer your home! And you will leave . . . that child for me to raise. She is no longer yours. She was born on this land. She belongs to us . . . the owners of this land."

Always laughed. "This land isn't not all yours. This land is mine, Miz Loretta. My sold babies bought most all this land. You ain't bought nothin!" She put her hand on Apple's head. "This child's daddy bought all that part of the left acres and part of the bottom land. It's more hers than yours."

Loretta screamed, "I will have Jason put you off!"

Always stepped back down the last step. "This is my land. I ain't goin nowhere, no time, no how. She started off, stopped, said, "You want them potatoes peeled, you peel em, eat your own dinner. I'll eat at my own house." She grabbed Apple's hand and walked calmly to the corner of the house; once around it and out of Loretta's sight, she broke into a run and ran all over the plantation screaming, "We free! We free! We free!"

My heart, or whatever it is, was shouting for joy too. Oh, if I just coulda been there with my babies. I thought of how my other children would be takin this and fore I knew it I was gone where Peach was.

Peach was just poring over one of many newspapers what hadn't got this final news yet. Her white maid was tryin to help her dress for some ball or nother. When I was leavin, she was askin her husband for any news from America. He just held her tightly, then Peach forgot America and went on to the ball.

I flew to Sun. He was alone, by hisself, lookin off toward the southland. A newspaper laying at his feet. He was a man, but he was cryin. He was wealthy now, and loved, no need for me watchin him. I fled back to Always.

All this was quick as a cinch, so I found Always at the church. Ohhhh, but all the singin and shouting them people was doin! Glad! Happy! Out of their minds! Then, some of them still didn't blive it! Just couldn't hold such a big thought in their minds! It was unblivable! They all was huggin and kissin each other and strangers too! They had all them white folks' food there, for the homeless that been goin on a long time. Wasn't no real church buildin, just a shack, but God didn't get no greater praise from the biggest cathedral buildin in the world! Not that night! That's right!

People was runnin round in the roads, grabbin strangers, askin them where they came from, where they been, who they were, who they mama was. Folks was lookin for their kin, their blood. Some just sat cryin. Some couldn't stop laughin. Some just held themself and rocked to the songs as tears run down their faces, nary a sound comin from their lips. Scarred hands shook, scarred backs bent to give thanks in prayer. Scarred souls wept in prayers of gratefulness. Even in all this, there was dis-blivin in this freedom. Is it true? . . . Can it be true? Freedom? Freedom? Blong to yourself?

The scissor-sharpner man was there, sharin the joy cause now, he knew, he could stay free. He hadn't never been always sure just what would happen. Always looked at him differently and hard. She also noticed another man, quiet, off in a corner, tired, sore and underfed, new here at this place. He wasn't sayin nothin, but you could see he was feelin great big feelins.

Always, and Apple, had never been lowed to go to church before. They just hugged everybody, laughed or cried with them, strangers and all, askin where they come from and did they know a Peach or a Sun, or her little children grown big now. Nobody, not one person, knew nothin!

Finally, returnin to her shack, she lay down and cried, thinkin of her family, her blood, as gone. All spread out and gone, all but that blood of hers in the main house, Loretta, and her son, Sephus, therefore, her blood in Apple. She hugged the child tight to hurtin, fell asleep and dreamed of me, sweet Jesus. Me and Doak Jr. and the land got all mixed up in it. She woke to the sound of big, heavy, fat raindrops on her tin roof, down on the land. She lay there thinkin, wonderin bout freedom.

She looked for Poon to come, to talk. But Poon stayed in that little house with Masr Jason, doin all the things she ever had, no change at all. You see? She loved Masr Jason. He was hers, place of all her children gone. Yet . . . yet, her mind kept pricklin up, to go to see could she find her sold children. Mayhap they was lookin for her. They was free now. Freedom, freedom. The word would ring round in her head, then her heart would like to start bustin for joy, then her fear, or somethin, would come to make her fraid. Freedom, the word rang in her head. She did not know just what to do with this freedom. But, one thing she did know, she was glad, was happy, to have it come at last, before she had died and gone. But how to mix freedom and Masr Jason? Would he leave cause she was free? Should she leave cause she was free? But, where to go? She didn't know what to do bout this freedom.

Always layed round and dreamed and thought big thoughts for bout a week, then her garden called to her and she went back to carin for things, outside of freedom, but part of freedom. Loretta looked, from the house she had done locked herself in, through the windows at Always workin, and decided she had won. However, somethin in her mind said, "Watch careful now. Watch careful."

CHAPTER 13

NOW, AT LAST, the inevitable war was over. Doak Jr. came home, and not long after, Soon came. They had fought different wars. Both were stronger, larger, but different in every other way.

Doak Jr. had a good tan that seemed to just linger on him. Didn't go away. Soon was now free, again.

Doak Jr., a young, weary, thin, bitter man. He did not like Soon at all now. But it really wasn't Soon, it was just Black. Black against white. His mind didn't clear it that it wasn't Soon that had won, it was Black, North, and justice that had prevailed.

The day he returned, it was a dark, thunderous lightnin day. Doak Jr. came stragglin in by foot down the road towards the main house. He knew he was Master now of this land, but the large, gray-white house looked wary in the drenching rain, and alone. Just the way he felt. Things looked kinda bleak, but he knew, at least he hoped, there was money there to put him back on his feet, put the land back on its feet. He wanted to be rich again. Well, that's natural.

He thought of the slaves on the land, howsomever many might still be there. Soon came into his mind, he pictured him as tryin to be uppity now that he was free. He knew Soon would be back cause his mother, Always, was there. But was she there? Probly gone runnin off with all the rest of them no-count niggas who probly flew the coop soon as they heard bout freedom. No more work outta them lessen they paid now.

Doak stamped his muddy boots on the front steps fore he realized wasn't nobody there to clean up the mess. He walked to the side entrance to the house. Loretta had heard him at the front and run there to see why the commotion. No one there, she ran to the side door to see Doak comin in. She stopped in her tracks as he looked up. They just looked at each other, these two white people whose lives was in such upheaval. At the same time, for the first time, they knew they was allies. They wasn't sure who was sposed to be boss of the money, if there was any. Doak knew he would be the one tho. After all, he was the man.

Then Loretta ran to him, hugged him, cried, took his wet things off, made him sit by the fire with a big drink. He dried off as they talked. He brought her up to date. Then she brought him up to date.

He learned Always was still there. His uncle still workin the farm, such as it was, but it was doin alright. The money. The money was gone, moved. She didn't tell him bout the sum she had put by over the years. Half the slaves gone, half stayed. No tellin who took the money. There was other money in the bank, but heard tell it wasn't no good no more. Only gold was good. Course,

Always had been one of them that knew where most the gold had been.

He ate a hot meal, the first in a long time. Then he went to sleep, sleep. Restless, but restful.

Loretta stood at the different windows lookin out over the land, thinkin, thinkin, bout how she was gonna make it. She didn't want to be birthed, live, and die all in this poor southern country. Mainly on her mind was where was the money? Her mind sped to Always. Always to Always. But, she smiled, Doak would take care of her. He was a man now, a strong man, and what he had seen in the war would make him a hard man to deal with. And he was hungry. Hungry for everything, she could see that. She might have to look out for herself sometimes, tho, gainst Doak.

Doak woke barely refreshed, but eager to get on bout the farm business. He inspected the farm, talked at long length with Jason. Checked the measly livestock. Noted with pleasure Always's garden.

CHAPTER 14

THE RAIN HAD STOPPED SOME, but was still drizzlin when he went into Always's chicken house shack, knockin as he went. She looked up and lit up, then her lights went down low, cause she could see he had somethin on his mind sides tellin her he was home safe.

She pointed to her only stool and he sat down in the dim lamp-lit room and watched her closely as they talked. She was still the dear woman who had helped raise him, but she was also a negress, the enemy.

Always was so proud and glad to have her son back, well, alive.

He spoke softly. "Ah . . . Always, if I members correctly, you the one person knew everything there was to know bout my father's plantation, his land and some of his business."

"Yes suh."

He shifted on the stool. "It is just right likely you know what happened to the money was buried round here, made and kept by my daddy for the care taken of this here land. For his heirs."

"Yes suh. I knowed most the place money was buried cause I help bury it with em."

Doak couldn't keep that note of anger comin into his voice tho it wasn't exactly aimed at Always. "Well . . . it seem that money, that gold, is gone now."

"Yes suh. I done heard of it."

Doak waited for her to say more. She didn't. "Well . . . as a reliable slave . . ." He stopped. ". . . person in my family, you should ought to know more bout what happened to it. I need to try to get it back where I can fix our house up here and get to work on makin this land pay again. I need money to do that."

Always moved a few things round on that little lopsided table she had under the one window, thinkin. She had planned this way head of time, should he come home safe. "I know one place where nobody did find, where there is some gold money." Doak jumped lightly. She said, "I will show you that when night falls."

Doak stood. "Show me now."

So, Always got two shovels and took him way down by the creek overhung with the wild trees full of birds, possums and squirrels. They walked in silence, Always steady watchin him from behind where she was walkin, fillin her eyes with her son and her pride. "Thank you God, he safe," she thought over and over.

Finally she stopped, reached out a hand to touch him. Lookin round carefully, she said, "We digs here."

They dug in the light rain til a spade hit a hard sound, then Doak got down on his knees and dug with his hands til he uncovered a small chest. He pulled it up and worked it open with his knife and fists. There was gold and silver. He looked up at Always, who was smilin.

"Is this all my daddy saved? All them years?"

"No such, there was more . . ."

"Where?" His tone was hard.

"Don't know where now. Can try to find out. I needs time."

Doak stood, holdin on to the chest. "You find out and you will never have to worry bout a home the rest of your life. I'll see to that my damn self!"

Now, Always had been enjoyin the doin of these things with her son. Feastin her eyes on him as they worked together. Her hands wantin to touch him. Her arms wantin to hold him. But now, her mind came to itself. "Yes suh. That's somethin I wants to talk bout with you."

"Well," he declared, "we done talked. You have a home here for as long as you want it . . . do you find me that gold."

Always rubbed the mud from her hands. "Yes suh. But I has somethin I wants to talk to you bout. I wants a place of my own. All my own."

Doak took a deep breath to keep his patience

up with this nigga. "Well, I ain't got much money but we can even find you a little ole place to live out your years in . . . in peace . . . do you find me that gold." The birds were now shrilling, screeching at the intruders. Thunder was heard off in the sky. Water just layin on the air, steady. They looked at each other, hard. She didn't turn away like he half expected.

They walked back carryin and draggin the heavy, small chest. They finally got back to Always's cabin. He was goin on with his load. Always turned to him. "Please, Masr Doak, come in one more time. I wants to say somethin to you."

Doak was eager to be home to count his gold and his future. But he thought of the other gold and drug the chest in and sat on the three-legged stool again with one foot on the small chest. "Well, Always?"

Now Always took a deep breath, looked out her small shack window at the rain drizzlin down on the green, green trees puffed up with water, trees she had done planted. All her life, all her grown life, she had lived here, slaved here, give birth here, cried here, died a thousand times here, buried in loneliness here. Worked, worked, worked here. Lost her children here. Here. She looked at her son, thinkin, "Gave birth to you here. Now you gon take the gold and give me a home for my life. When I die, I be all gone and won't stand for nothin cept I been blonged to you and your daddy."

She took another deep breath, sighed, said, "Old Masr Perkins done died. His widder, Miz Perkins, done died too. They done left that Perkins plantation crost the way, empty and goin down to ruin."

Doak spoke, impatient. "Yes, yes, that's too bad. Mayhap I can buy it up and add to my land. That is why I need that gold so bad, Always! Now is the time to get richer, get ahead! Add to what we, my daddy, done already done! Do you understand that?"

Always nodded her head slowly. "I wants to live there. Cross the way from you'll."

Doak laughed softly, but wildly. "Oh, is that what this is bout? Well, if I can buy it, of course you can live there and take care it for me! Long as you want to." He smiled.

Always turned to him directly. "No suh. What I mean, I wants to live there . . . and die there . . . as on my own land."

Doak frowned. "Well, that takes money. And what would you do with a place even that size? Must be a hundred acres."

Always frowned. "I took care of this here place and this'n is bigger."

Doak held his hand up. "You had overseein and help, white help, white leaders. My daddy was runnin this place, you just worked . . ."

Always shook her head slowly. "Naw suh. I took care this place, me and Masr Jason. Cause your daddy was a fool."

Doak stood. "Now Always, don't get beyond yourself, even if you is free now."

Always stood her ground. "Tellin you the truth. I'm the reason you got that gold there." She pointed to the chest at his feet. Doak looked down at the chest, then slowly up at Always.

Always went on talkin, "I done worked enough for you to give me my own place . . . suh."

Doak, his lips tight. "There is not enough money for me to buy that plantation for you and do things for myself too! Sides, it ain't fittin for me to have to buy you no house. You was bought and paid for, that's why you worked."

Always, head bowed, looked up. "When we finds that other gold?"

Doak stepped closer to Always. "You already know where that gold is, don't you?"

"I'm gonna see if'n I do."

Doak glowered. "You are tryin to deal, to bargain with me! A white man!? You are a nigga slave tryin to be smart! And a woman, too!"

"Just tryin to live, suh."

"You get me that gold or you won't have no life left to live, niggah!"

Always sighed deep. "Don't talk to your mama like that son. I . . . I could call you them same names . . . but I ain't."

Doak laughed, ugly. "Just cause you raised me . . ."

Always looked in his eyes. "Done more than raised you. Birthed you."

Disbelief and insult all over his face. "Birthed me?"

Always looked steady at him. "Birthed you."

She pointed at her cot. "Right on that cot in this shack."

Doak forgettin to be quiet. "What are you talkin bout, crazy nigga woman? I am a white man! I know my mother!"

Always didn't fear. "You know the mother I gave you."

Doak, "YOU gave me?"

Always still spoke softly, but firm. "The woman you think is your mama did birth a son that same time. You both had the same daddy. You looked much alike. So I gave her my son. To be sure you wouldn't not be a slave. Would live right. I took her son . . . and raised him as mine."

Doak instantly thought of Soon.

Always continued softly, even with love. "I am your natchel-born mama."

Doak reach out and slapped my Always so hard, so hard. She didn't do nothin. He said, "You spect me to blive you my mama? Just like that? So you can use me? You are crazy!"

"Can prove it, son."

Doak, about to leave, froze in his bent position to pick up the chest. "Prove it?"

Always nodded her head. "Can prove it."

"How can you prove such a thing? A lie? A black lie?"

Always pointed at her son. "God gave us somethin . . . to prove it. A sign."

Doak wanted to snarl. "A sign? What sign can prove you, black as you is, is my rightful mama!?"

Always stepped back in the small space, lifted her dress to her breast, pulled her underdrawers down enough to show her mole. Doak stared at her first in more than dismay, disbelief. Then, he went into shock. His mind exploded a little.

Always held the mole in sight. "I knows God gived you one just like it, in the same place. That marks you for mine. My own son."

Doak put his hand on his hip over his own mole, stared at this slave who was his mama and howled. "I won't, I can't . . . I'm not your son! I'm not your son, black bitch!"

Always reached out to him. "Don't talk to your mama like that, son. Yes suh, you my son. Black man, you my son."

Doak saw red everywhere in his head. His hands reached out and caught Always round the neck.

He flung her down and leaned over her to kill her. They struggled. She was strong. He was young, but tired. They looked in each other's eyes as they silently fought, each to win. He wanted to rid hisself of this ugliness that called itself his mother, who could ruin his life, his dreams. Change his world. Always fought cause she had always had to fight to live, this was just another time to get pass.

Her throat almost closed, she whispered, "Son, don't kill me. God won't never forgive you."

His horror told him, "Fuck god."

Her mind was workin fast as it could for her dear life. God didn't work, so, "You ain't never gonna find out all where that gold is, do I die, son."

Doak glared at her with hatred, but he loosened his grip on her throat. She took his hands firmly and pulled them from her neck, steady lookin at him in the eyes. "I blive I know how I can find out where it is. I blive I can." He raised off from her slowly. She pulled herself to her feet, shaking her head, gettin her breath, thinkin, all at the same time.

197

Doak, breathin hard, said, "You get me my gold. I'll let you live, but don't you never tell them words out loud again!"

Always moved to the far corner of the little shack. "I the onliest chanst you have to get that gold. Don't put your hands on me no more again. And if you don't help me, your mama, out of the kindness in your heart . . . then help me cause I will tell Loretta and everyone else . . . And they will listen to me. You can't cut that mole out, cause it will only leave another scar. So YOU IS MY SON."

Doak stood there with hate written all over his face, tears runnin down it too.

Always stepped toward him, then stopped herself. "I don't never need to tell nobody. I wants you to keep on livin good and fine. Just . . . I want to live good too. Just help your mama, son, help me get away too. They will let you buy that land and give it to me cause they blive you white and you can do whatever you wants to."

Doak thought again of killin her. When he spoke his voice was full of tears, hatred, and despair as he jerked his shoulder away from her reach. "I don't have enough money."

Always's voice broke. "I done save my own money over these years. Don't need you to spend all yours."

He looked up eagerly now. "You know where that gold is, don't cha?"

"I'm gonna try findin out. But I still gots my own money, son. Is we got a understandin of what we both us want to do? I will find you more gold. Not tell nobody you is my own son. I will move crost the road a way, you don't have to see me no mo. You just do the legal papers for me. That's all I's askin."

Doak Jr., beaten, "I . . . I'm goin to the house."

Always, hopin, "I's gonna count on you, son."

"Don't ever call me son again."

"Done called you son all your little life."

Doak started through the little door. Always spoke urgently. "Soon, soon, soon. We got no time to waste. That land be gone."

Doak threw back to her, "I'll think on it . . . when the rain stop. When you get me that gold."

"Whatsomever you say, son. But weather ain't got nothin to do with my life. Ain't never matter to nobody before. But if you say so, I'll wait. I'll wait to try to find the gold too. The best be for me to do it soon befo somebody done took it off, too. Like they can do that Perkins land I wants."

Doak looked at Always over his shoulder, was hunched up with carryin that chest. With hatred and respect. "Awright. I'm goin today bout the land. But you get out and find that gold today too!"

"Yes suh, son. Yes suh." She shut the door softly and slowly, then sat down on her cot and cried and cried. Cried with relief. Somethin off her shoulders after all the years of burden.

She had not known exactly what her plan was all these years, but it was workin out. It was maybe gonna work out.

Later in the day, when the drizzlin had stopped, tho the dark clouds remained in the sky, Always went walkin to relieve her tight nerves. She had never gone this far with nobody before in a thinkin game of life. She walked over the land, thinkin and talkin to herself.

She reached down to the rich black earth and took up a handful. She stared at it, rollin it round in her hands. She looked up to the heavens. "Lord, do freedom mean I got to leave my home? This my home too. Where else I'm gonna go? Where else lay my tired body down if not here where it got tired. Here, where my dead sister and baby is layin dead at? All my babies you done give me . . . been sold by this master to buy this land. This land I hold here in my hand. If that don't make it mine, Lord, what do? What make it his? Thems? Cause he own me? Naw Lord, naw Lord, you ain't be no way like that." She started to cryin and runnin round them fields, lookin up at the Lord sometime. "My blood done ran out on this ground. My tears done run down on it. My sweat done built it up. Done fed us all. Don't that make it mine too, Lord? I hurt all over my body cause of this land, Lord. My feelins is used up over this land, Lord. WHO can tell me to go? Don't you. Don't you Lord, please."

Always was runnin, cryin, stoopin to pick up that dirt and crush it to her breast. I ached for her, and I understood.

She went on and on. "I didn't want to come . . . I came. I came, worked, cried and slaved. I came and now they want me to go. I'm stayin, Lord. Stayin here, if they don't get me my land. I's tried to find in somewheres in me to call some place other Home. I can't, Lord. I know this dirt like my own blood runnin in my body. Like my own heart bein inside my chest. Like my hands and feet. My body don't stop, Lord. This land is part of my body. My roots is deep in this ground. I came, they bought me, I slaved here, This my land. Even freedom, sweet as it be, ain't gonna make me leave this land. It mine, Lord. Now, it mine, Lord, I ain't never gonna go. You hear me, Lord?" She raised the dirt to the sky, tears flowin. "It mine, it be mine, it be me, Lord! Sho! Just like you done give me my life, now my life is mine, so is this here land. It mine. I tell you it MINE! LORD! Or give me some land of my own self I can call my home."

CHAPTER 15

SHE WOULDN'T GIVE Doak any more gold except for the amount needed to buy the Perkins land. She had to keep tellin him he would get the rest of his when hers was all set. Doak grew to hate her more. He tried to plan some way to kill her. But the gold! He felt like the slave! So he did her biddin . . . and grew to respect her more. But he never thought of her as his mother.

It was good she could read cause he woulda fooled her with them deeds. But she could read.

She saved herself. Doak was all times amazed with her sense. When he finally got the gold she was gonna give him, she was through with needin him and stayed way from him, til she felt time could smooth him down.

The land bought and hers, she took to roundin up old slaves and young, promisin them a home if they help her fix her place up. They knew how to do most everything. People in the stores thinkin she buyin for Doak Jr. gave her the best at a good price.

Her place was goin to be nice. She furnished it with the best of things, tho she never lowed no one in them special rooms. She didn't much go in em herself cept to go sit and look round at what was hers. Hers.

She had long ago started goin round that church house and keepin her eye on that quiet Tim. He watched her too. One day they was told to hold hands in a circle and sing together. He came to where she was and held her hand tightly, she held his tightly back and they almost never did let go, even when the meetin was over. Finally they did tho.

One day, when she had made up her mind on him, she smiled at him and took his hand again. He smiled back and left his hand in hers. In a quiet, sort of slow way, wary, timid love peeked above the soil of their hearts, lookin round to see was it a rocky place.

Always wanted to move quick tho. She asked him, "Is you a married man?"

Tim answered, "Was."

"What is you now?"

"Cain't find my wife, my woman."

"She sposed to be round here?"

"Naw, I don't guess now."

"Well, how you gonna find her stayin in one place?"

"Done foun somethin else."

"What you think you done found?"

"You?"

"You ain't too bashful, is you?"

"Cain't hep it, no how."

"What you mean to do with me? I ain't no easy woman."

"Don't want none."

"What you to doin with me?"

"What kin I do wit you?"

"I'll think on it."

"I likes that." Then he moved slowly away. Smilin.

The scissor-man was long gone out of her mind. She had been goin to marry him for livelihood and security, she thought. The way she felt about Tim . . . was love. Her first real love. Now that she was free, and he was free, their love was free to give to each other. And they did.

They took their time, but not a lot of time cause they didn't have much time. Always had most moved into her new house as it was movin along and now she was ready for marriage. Tim had been helpin, but mostly he was a livestock worker with just general knowledge of buildin a house, like them little shotgun houses for the tenant farmers on her new land.

They waited for their lovin. Didn't make none. Wanted it all right, marriage and all, for the first time in all their lives. The day came, at last. Always had on a white weddin dress she made herself. Tim had on a brand-new blue suit. Flowers was everwhere. Even vegetables was set up in bouquets when the flowers ran out. Cause that's what she raised was vegetables, you see? The peoples was there, ex-slaves now tenants on her farm. After the bride kissed the groom and laughed out loud, too long, cause she was so happy, everybody had a good time bein free. They ate her good cookin and drank some of the homemade wine Tim had made. A few others at the weddin got so mixed up in all that love they was tryin to find somebody to marry while the preacher was there. It was romantic, you see.

The night of Always's weddin. The weddin night.

Everything was new in their new bedroom. Seem like even they was new. Magine! Two slaves in a real house. THEIR house! Picked each other out to love. And DID IT! Never before in either of each life had they ever been able to make such a choice. And no other slave they knew of! Chile, that freedom is something!

They was both shy, kinda bashful, tho Lord knows, they both had been through so much of life. Seen so much. Been made to do so much.

Now . . . they had love . . . and everything.

They lay side by side, holdin hands. When they talked, they almost whispered.

"I is your real wife now."

"I knows, an I is proud."

"You sho you loves me?"

"Bout too late if I wan't sho."

"Ain't talkin bout time! I wants to be real loved."

"I loves you, too. Real love."

"I feel like this my first time at lovin."

"Is our first time at lovin. First time at bein married, sides with a broom. I's yours. We's together. Woman and man. Man and wife."

"Man and wife! By a preacher. Like white folks, Tim."

"Like real peoples sposed to be, everywhere."

"Our folkses wasn't there. My mama wasn't there. She dead. Where your mama, Tim?"

His whisper dropped. "I nevah knew my mama. Nevah had none."

"Never had no mama? Ohhhh, Tim."

"You my everythin, Always. You my wife, my mama, my baby, my woman. My everythin."

"Tim? When you was undressin? I saw them scars on your back."

"They's the las ones. Won't be no mo."

"I's gonna rub em down with my special linment."

"Yo special linment is love. You done already rubbed me all over my heart and soul. My body be awright now."

They was quiet awhile, just layin there bein together. Then Tim said, "I didn't see no scars on yo back."

"Mos my scars is in my mind. Can't see em clear."

Tim raised his head a little. "Then how I'm gon help em go away?"

Always turned her face to him. "Tim, you done soothed my scars with your love and kindness and goodness."

She unclasped their hands. "Put your hand on my stomach."

He did. "Sho feel like a pretty stomach."

"I's lovin you, Tim, and you betta treat me right, love me back, good and strong."

"Yo knows that or we wouldn't be layin here now."

They laughed and he began to rub her stomach. She whispered closer to his ear. "You feels good to me, Tim."

He smiled to hisself. "Ahhhhh, you sho feels good to me. Did from the first time I seen you in that church."

She raised her head a little. "Reckon God done blessed us cause we met in the church?"

"Always, I'm blessed. I'm blessed. And it feel so good to be blessed."

"Where you goin with your hand, Tim?"

"Home. My new home. I's bringin myself home to you."

"Come on home then. Home is waitin for you."

"Fo me always?"

"Always for you, always."

And as he tenderly passed one strong arm under her body and pulled her gently under him, they kissed and he whispered into her mouth, "Ahhhh, I loves yo, Always, I loves yo."

And they came together in marriage. They

made a home. And it wasn't too long fore they made a baby, chile.

Oh! My! My! How much we slaves, of all colors, have missed. Oh! My! I never did get to feel nothin like that. There ain't nothin, NOTHIN, like you wantin somebody and them wantin you. Loving. Lovin somebody! Just really nothin like makin love to somebody you love, when you BOTH want to and you together doin it! Oh! My! My! Well, that's what they had, when they was freed.

Always wanted a black child by a black man. And she went to workin on it right away. Tim loooved his wife. That's why it wasn't long fore Always was pregnant. I was excited cause this child we could keep. It was ours!

When Always had their son, Tim stayed at her side long as she would let him. It was the first time she had ever had help havin a baby. It was the first time she could look up at its daddy, hold his hand, and wait for their child of love to be born. If you ain't never had that happen, or helped it happen, chile, you don't know what love is when you have a child.

When Always and Tim had got married, they had to decide on a last name of their own choice. They pondered many hours. They finally decided on "More" cause Always say that's what they want! When the baby was born, Always say she want to name him "Master," so everybody have to call him Master. Tim just went long with things, thinkin he could name the next ones. But there never was no next one. Master More had to carry on the name all by hisself. And he ended up doin it in a big way, too. But, I'll tell you all that when I get to it. In the meantime, their farm prospered, with Always addin things along the way. She always thought of gold.

Tim and Always built more shacks for the ex-slaves and gave them to them for life, long as they worked til they couldn't. She encouraged them to have gardens of their own, thereby saving her stuff for market.

When she would send them out to do outside work for white people, she gave them 90 percent of their money, so they would be free, on their own.

She still had some gold, so she bought two carriages and rented them out with a well-dressed driver to ladies who wanted to be ladies goin in style to local events, but who had lost most of their genteel money. She paid the drivers and kept the rest, naturly.

Tim raised the stock and they both ran the farm. They prospered.

Across the road a way, Doak Jr. also prospered. He yet glared cross the road at her, but she had given him the most of his gold, so he had no real fuss, just felt bested. Loretta, even tho her house was bein fixed and built up and beautified, yet looked cross the road at Always darkly. Not hatin her so much tho. Close kin, yet far apart from love.

Doak Jr. found him a pretty little wife, blue-eyed and blond, just as cute as she could be. Smart. Nice. Good-hearted. She fell in love with Apple and had her often, everyday, to their house, much to the pleasure of Loretta. Probly what helped

Loretta stop hatin Always so much. Loretta could watch her own child grow, and she did love Apple. Apple loved all the good things happenin to her. Lovely little clothes, good food, tender care. She was growin up to be a mighty pretty girl and it was good for her to have others lovin her, cause Always was taken up with her new son fore long. Little Apple was thinkin she was in love with Soon. He was too old for her, but she had that feelin for him girls have for grown-ups sometimes. Loretta was plannin, strongly, for to send Apple off to the North to school. Apple was learnin good already, studyin hard, Loretta teachin her. Loretta was a natural born teacher it seemed. Loretta knew Apple loved Soon. Loretta didn't want Apple marryin no black man, so everything she did was to gear Apple toward the North. She put dreams in her head and they worked. I'm glad. Give everybody a future if you can.

Soon didn't get married right away. He worked with his mama, Always, and commence to pile up a good piece of homeland for hisself. He say he want his wife from somewhere not in the South. Said he would wait awhile.

CHAPTER 16

I WAS GETTIN mighty tired, weak. Always's new baby, Master, was growin slowly. I'd have to wait years to see his life. I wanted to, but I was so tired.

I drifted off to Peach, I thought for the last time. She was tryin to visit the United States. Her family didn't want her to go. Her husband specially. She wanted to go see and find her first family. He told her she had her family there with him. I could see she was goin to get her way. He told her she had to take one of their own children with her, and she had to stay white while she was there. See and leave!

Well, I ain't gonna take up no lotta time tellin you bout her trip. Once she got to the South, it wasn't no time fore she found Always on accounta Loretta bein so close to her. And when Loretta saw Peach! Chile! Peach couldn't stay no white woman then if Loretta had not wanted her to, but Loretta thought of Apple and that made it easy for Peach.

Loretta decided she wanted Apple to go to school in Scotland and Always decided she wanted Soon to go somewhere for some special education in Europe, wherever Peach thought best. Peach was way more than happy to do all these things cause she had done missed havin colored people somewhere around her. It gets to be that way sometime. And tho they was mostly white, they was still black. They got all that settled for when the time came.

Soon was not too eager to leave all that he was workin on for hisself, but he wasn't no fool and he did want somethin better and he wanted a wife from somewhere else. He, too, liked his relative and her daughter she brought with her. Pretty chile.

But let me tell you bout when Always and Peach met again.

Always thought it was some rich woman comin to see bout her carriages. She was bendin down round some of them special plants of hers and stood up waitin for Peach to get to her. Peach broke into a run, cause that chile hadn't done changed much inside herself. She was truly glad to see her sister, her own first family. They hugged and held on to each other . . . so long, oh, so long. Squeezin, cryin . . . oh, so long. My family, my blood.

Always wanted to be mad cause she had done been left down there to fend for herself in the madness of slavery. Wanted to know why somebody didn't try to come back and help her, buy her. All Peach answered was, "Because I couldn't! Wasn't any way I could have done it, with my husband and my family. I didn't know anything about passage, buyin and not getting recognized and whatever all else there is. So there! I'm back now to do whatever I can do, so we can be together again as a family. You can't come to Scotland. But I can take little Apple with me and anybody else that looks white." Well, truth is the light. Right or wrong.

I had done dropped over to see Sun. He was gettin ready to go down to see bout his sisters too. He got there whilst Peach was there. Chile, I'm tellin you! I was so happy, so glad, so full up with joy! To see my childrens together again. Mine. But my joy wasn't no bigger than theirs was.

Plum was the only sadness in their hearts. When Sun got there, he found em the same way Peach had done. Always took them to Plum's grave place. Only people she ever did take sides Tim and Master. They held each other and cried some more. Chile, slavery was hard, hard on a body in so many ways. These blood of mine was way more than lucky and blessed.

Sun and Peach argued bout Soon and Apple and it ended up with Soon goin with Sun. Sun didn't care what nobody thought, but he didn't want to be found out to be black yet either. Soon was just as glad either way. His mama would look out for his things while he was gone to get a education to be a vet . . . tin . . . nary. That's what he had done decided while he was talkin and workin with Peach. See, Always put everybody to work. Now he knew he could visit in Scotland whenever he wanted to anyway.

Chile, I'm tellin you this FREEDOM was really somethin if you had any sense to work with it! My chile, Always, had planned when she didn't even know she was plannin!

CHAPTER 17

LORETTA HAD TO COME to Always when Sun was home. Always treated her like the lady she was cause now she knew more bout how Sun had got away. Loretta was very polite. Her face just lit up when she saw Sun. After all these years! She, in the end, wanted him to take Apple, but Apple was settled. It was all alright.

She and Sun talked for such a long while. This time he did invite her up to his home as a relative from the South. When she left and went home cross the road, her mind was full of dreams of the new men she would meet and perhaps marry. The clothes she would have, the places she could go. Looked like this life was just payin off for everybody.

Doak Jr. just wouldn't let none of em over to his house and Loretta never could figure why. He didn't like Always and he didn't want nothin to do with none of em, don't care how white and light their skin was! He didn't want to be caught lookin like them, you see? Not be close to black, no way!

I was just gettin more tired and tired. I just began to drift off and drift off to places I didn't even think of.

One day, in my driftin, I passed a ocean. Big ole thing. Strong winds blowin, beautiful sand glistenin in the sun. Birds flyin all over all round me. The trees bowin to the wind, even growin that way. I stopped to rest under one of them trees.

You know what I did? I fell into a deep, deep sleep. So peaceful, so restful I slept I don't know how long, chile! When I finally woke, I blive it was cause of the noise of war. It was so many years later. It was bout fifty years later!

I rushed, I flew to where I had last seen Always and Master. Things had changed so much, oh, how things had changed.

Always was dyin. Old, old and dyin. So I knew this was the end for me too. My children had grown and now their children was grown. Master had children of his own and he was dead already. He left two boys and two girls, grown.

Soon had come back and now he was dead. His white wife too. They had left one boy and one girl, Edward Soon and Edna, grown.

Apple never did come back cept for visits, quick visits. She lived in England with a English husband, her children, Alice and Gary, was grown too and she was gettin on old. She had money tho, she had learned well from Always.

I didn't get up to see bout Peach cause she was still livin, old. I knew I had a little time to see her. Her children was everywhere, Ireland, France, Spain, everywhere, livin white. I knew Sun was dead just from thoughts floatin round.

I went to Always to be with her whilst she died. Wondered would we get to talk now since we both gonna be dead. Tim was long dead now, too. He left beautiful memories tho, cause Always never married again. He did see his grandchildren.

I must tell you this tho. Doak Jr. had got mos all that land back from Always, in one way or another. After Tim died she let down on her watchfulness. Even some of the slaves and their children she had taken on, had done unkind things to her. Stealin. White folks stealin too, once they found out that the land was hers and not Doak's. Doak helped them cause he still held enmity cause she bested him. When Doak died he was ragin and ravin, confused. But he had had a good, full life with his sweet wife who died soon after he did. They left children.

A real white man, Jared, had come to Doak Jr. and his oldest son. Doak the third or fourth, I don't know. He was tired of bein poor and seein black folks with things he couldn't get. He hadn't tried workin harder. He had thought of a way he had heard of where white folks rode in the night and killed black folk and took from them.

Changed records and stole from them. Now, all them white folks was not this way. Some would never have thought of this kind of thing, but poor white ignorant have-nothin folks thinks of anything. This man, Jared, did think of ways to rid blacks of all what they could. Even burn em out!

He needed somebody with some respect, tho, to get the main folks he needed to help this idea along. Doak Jr. had not done never thought of this, but if he refused it, he knew they would wonder why, cause he was always seeming to help that black woman, Always, crost the way. He didn't want no reason, no way for nobody to think him no more than a nice white man helpin a nigga who had raised him, so he agreed. Only if they was not killed, he said. Don't kill em, just take all they got. Burn houses down, that's alright. Steal horses, cows, hogs, food, whatever you want, but don't kill em.

It didn't work out that way, cause it never does with somebody with a ugly, mean, jealous mind. Jared had that kind of mind. UGLY. He took to wearin them sheets he had done heard of, gettin other jealous whites to follow him. And the Ku

Klux Klan came to be in that region. Always suffered. In fact that is how Tim died. Fightin for his wife and life.

A lot of other blacks suffered too, cause what could you do? Everybody with some power was now joined into it, almost. Only a few with a conscience was not. And how many people you know got a conscience?

It grew, it done grown even up til now. Still goin, but let me get back to Always and all she tried to get and keep in the right way. Gold, silver and all, she worked for it. Didn't ride no horses in the night under no cover-up sheet to steal. Worked on her son only. And you might say he owed her that. But he didn't think so. He would sit up in church, even, and listen to that gospel music and think, with malice, what she had done to him. Ain't some people fools? He was free on count of her. Maybe a whole lot of other white-lookin men and women are free that way too, and they don't know it. Who knows? Maybe they do know it.

But his concentration was on Always. What she

had. Even if he didn't need it. He didn't want to see her with it. Chile, the man ended up ownin so much they named the town after him. Butler-town. It was his town, he was so rich! He had plenty to leave to his children. A whole town practcly. Still, he wanted back what he felt Always had taken from him.

They didn't get it all, howsomever. She held on to the main parts. She even still had some gold buried, and now nobody knew where it was. She only woulda told Tim, which she did, and Master, and they was both gone. It was buried deep under the ground in Tim's old wine cellar.

Her four grandchildren was there. Grown. Waitin for her to die, so they could get on bout their business. Well . . . two loved their gramma Always. One middle one, Peter, and the youngest, named after Peach.

Peter had been educated and he was followin his uncle Soon's steps in the vet . . . tin . . . nary. Peach was a teacher and yet loved the South, so she planned to stay on in her grandmother's house that the other two wanted to sell. She had done fallen in love with one of them husky dark men behind a plow, Carl. She was gonna stay and get him. He seem to be glad bout that.

The other two, Rich and Rita, was back from some city they had done gone to after they was educated and they wanted to get on back to civilization, they said.

So that's where I was. Still with my family. Blood so many places I couldn't never more keep up with it. Wouldn't know some pieces of my family if they stepped into my eyes.

When my beloved daughter Always closed her eyes and rested her soul, she didn't come to me. She passed me by. Oh Lord.

Now . . . I figured I'd go somewhere and lay down and close my eyes and be gone too. I'm shame to tell you, but that ain't what happened. I tried my best to get on way from here. Tired of livin without livin. But try as I might, I didn't go nowhere. Just fell asleep again. Short nap. Woke up fifteen years later, bout 1933 or so. Didn't know nowhere else to go, so went back to Always's house.

You know what I found? Like to saw history

repeatin itself! I said to myself, things got to get better somehow! Everything looked so peaceful on the top. I happen to stay round just long nough to try to enjoy some of that peace, then when I saw what all was under that peace, I HAD to stay round to see what would happen again, to my blood. My blood. My family.

You all had had wars and famines, depressions and recessions, union fights, labor horrors, poverty worse, look like, then some slavery. For all colors this time! People was catchin hell and didn't have to die to do it!

Them men up there in them high offices, all over the world, was still lyin to you all. You all was lettin em then. It ain't changed too much now!

Time. Time and life. They moves on. History don't repeat itself, people repeat themselves! History couldn't do it if you all didn't make it. Time don't let you touch it tho. God was wise. He sure knew what he was doin! Cause you all is reachin for the moon! Done got there! If the sun wasn't so hot . . . God knew what he was doin then too, cause, see, life depends on the sun.

They call Time a old man. But Time don't age,

ain't old. Every day is new. Don't nothin age but us and what we make. Wonder why? Time and Life. Well . . . Time takes care of everything . . . and it will take care of you.

I was so tired in my soul. Tired of all I had lived and seen, now, I was tired from all I had stayed round to see. I saw my blood spread out all over into all such places I never dreamed of in my wildest dreams. Makes me know, if from one woman all these different colors and nationalities could come into bein, what must the whole world be full of?!

Yet I found more strangeness in the lives of my new blood through my children. Always there tho, was love and fear, and hate lurkin behind. Some happiness. Some pain. Finally I even found some peace. But I'm gettin ahead of my story again.

I'm gettin tired too. And weaker. I seem to be fadin on way from here.

I want to stay . . . and I don't want to stay. To see what happens in this world so full of so many different colored people. But, I'm scared to see too much more. Such a wave of hate is being planted up deeper in the world. The devil is the busiest thing I know.

Some kin have been known to marry each other, or make sex and love. Well, life done proved it's some of everybody in this world, all colors.

It's some who tries to spread love . . . and, I think Love will always win. Always. But . . . what a fight it must make.

I thank God for the people in this here world that tries to spread love to all kind of people. Cause, chile, can you imagine what this world would be like without em?

All my family, my blood, is mixed up now. They don't even all know each other. I just hope they don't never hate or fight each other, not knowin who they are.

Cause all these people livin are brothers and sisters and cousins. All these beautiful different colors! We! . . . We the human Family. God said so! FAMILY!

J. CALIFORNIA COOPER is the author of three collections of stories, *Some Soul to Keep*, *Homemade Love* (a recipient of the 1989 American Book Award), and *A Piece of Mine*, as well as seventeen plays, many of which have been produced and performed on the stage, public television, radio, and college campuses. Her plays have also been anthologized, and in 1978 she was named Black Playwright of the Year for *Strangers*, which was performed at the San Francisco Palace of Fine Arts. Among her numerous awards are the James Baldwin Writing Award (1988) and the Literary Lion Award from the American Library Association (1988). Ms. Cooper lives in a small town in Texas, and is the mother of a daughter, Paris Williams.